What people are saying about …

God's ~~Not~~ Like That

"After decades of studying, teaching, and preaching, Bryan brings a wealth of wisdom and life experience to a timely and significant topic. He helps the reader go beyond the mere *acquisition* of information to the essential step of practical *application*. This unique resource has powerful insights that have the potential to make a meaningful difference in any life. It is a book you'll want to read more than once."

Gary J. Oliver, ThM, PhD, Going Deeper Together Ministries, professor of psychology and practical theology at John Brown University, author of over twenty books including *Mad About Us*

"In this book, Pastor Clark shows us that there is a relationship between the way we have been treated by our earthly father and the way we view our heavenly Father. He wisely counsels us to think rightly of our heavenly Father and we will receive the forgiveness, acceptance, and self-worth our earthly father failed to give us."

Erwin W. Lutzer, pastor emeritus at Moody Church, Chicago

"With wisdom and realism, Bryan Clark coaches us in understanding how deeply our families of origin have shaped not only who we now are but how we think of God. This biblical and accessible book will help any open-hearted reader peel back layers of misperception of what God is like, layers they didn't even realize were there. Thank you, Pastor Bryan."

Dane Ortlund, senior pastor of Naperville Presbyterian Church, author of *Gentle and Lowly* and *Deeper*

"Even as Christians, many of us have earthly father wounds that cripple our ability to trust the heavenly Father we endeavor to serve. For over two decades, Bryan Clark's solid biblical teaching and consistent walk as Christ's representative have cultivated deep healing for me, both personally and professionally. I'm excited to offer *God's Not Like That* to peers, colleagues, and clients as we work together to clarify and heal our misperceptions about the character and heart of God."

Lynette Erickson, MA, LPC, psychotherapist

"In *God's Not Like That*, Pastor Bryan Clark uses his vulnerability and transparency to help answer a lot of important questions that Christians struggle with. He breaks down each question very practically in a way you can understand it. I highly recommend this book to any Christian wanting a correct view of God."

Prince Amukamara, Super Bowl champion and
Nebraska Football Hall of Fame inductee

"Few books have captivated me with such an irresistible desire to read more, dig deeper, and explore my view of God. In a performance- and consumer-driven society, the revealing truth, that we are God's masterpieces and He views us that way, is affirming, revealing, and liberating. Reading *God's Not Like That* stirred me to reflect deeply, identify underlying messages, and extend grace as other books have not."

Katherine S. Ankerson, university administrator,
AIA, FIIDA, FIDEC, NCARB

"Bryan Clark has written a must-read for any follower of Jesus Christ. No matter who you are, the book speaks with biblical clarity, insightfulness, and compassion into your life. And as a pastor, I can't recommend this book enough for giving insights into shepherding people as they wrestle through not just their family of origin but, most importantly, their view of God."

Todd Nighswonger, lead pastor at
Cornerstone Church, Simi Valley, CA

"Bryan Clark has written a very helpful book that explains how our family of origin forms the basis of our beliefs about God. Coming from imperfect situations and being raised by imperfect people can leave us with distortions and misbeliefs about who God is and how He feels about us. Pastor Clark combines biblical truth and practical insight in providing an accurate picture of our heavenly Father. *God's Not Like That* is a valuable guide for all of us on this journey."

Meribeth Tenney, PhD, licensed psychologist

"Bryan Clark connects the dots between our view of God and family of origin. This book is a must-read for every Christian who struggles in their faith and needs answers."

Seth Gheen, ThM, chaplain

"Pastor Bryan Clark, in his whimsical, approachable manner, moves our common assumption that God is just like our dad or our worst boss. These impressions run deep for a reason. Prepare for depth and change both personally and communally with Pastor Bryan's insights and wisdom. This work speaks to new believers and old disciples alike. As our society constantly reshapes, this book couldn't come at a better time."

Jared Anderson, songwriter and worship leader

"What do we do when the Bible's teachings about God do not reconcile with how we feel in relationship to Him? Bryan directs us back to where we learn the most about God: our families of origin. In *God's Not Like That*, we study how God intentionally designed the family to reflect different aspects of His character, while concurrently examining how our experiences either affirmed truths about God or created barriers to fully trusting Him. If you have ever struggled with trusting God, this book is for you."

Lindsey Sauer, MA in community counseling
and MEd in higher education

"As Bryan unpacks the biblical role of family, as well as our need to connect with God, he speaks with compelling compassion and authority that are so needed today. I have seen him navigate the challenging, fulfilling, sometimes disappointing, and often unpredictable role of leadership in the church and his own family through many years. His life has demonstrated a deep dependence on God and His Word and shown a keen awareness of our desperate need for God's grace in everything he has faced. This book provides needed perspective and a practical, solid foundation in our uncertain and turbulent times."

Tim Bohlke, founder and director of Harbor Ministries

"*God's Not Like That* is a rich primer about God's creative and redemptive plan for humankind, lived out in a family context. Reflecting on my family's origin of spirituality, I recognized the tension between our genuine love of God and the tainted legalism we also followed. I believe this book will help us, and many others, grasp a more accurate and healthy view of God."

Dr. Brad Riddle, LIMHP

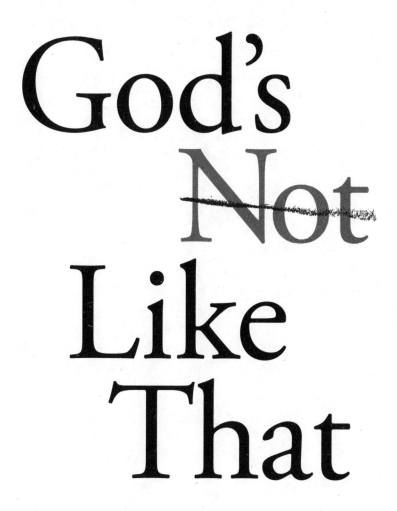

God's
~~Not~~
Like
That

Bryan Clark

God's Not Like That

Redeeming
Inherited Beliefs and
Finding the Father
You Long For

DAVID C COOK

transforming lives together

GOD'S NOT LIKE THAT
Published by David C Cook
4050 Lee Vance Drive
Colorado Springs, CO 80918 U.S.A.

Integrity Music Limited, a Division of David C Cook
Brighton, East Sussex BN1 2RE, England

The graphic circle C logo is a registered trademark of David C Cook.

The website addresses recommended throughout this book are offered as a
resource to you. These websites are not intended in any way to be or imply an
endorsement on the part of David C Cook, nor do we vouch for their content.

Unless otherwise noted, all Scripture quotations are taken from the (NASB®) New
American Standard Bible®, Copyright © 1960, 2020 by The Lockman Foundation.
Used by permission. All rights reserved. www.lockman.org. Scripture quotations
marked NIV are taken from the Holy Bible, New International Version®, NIV®.
Copyright © 1973, 2011 by Biblica, Inc.™ Used by permission of Zondervan. All
rights reserved worldwide. www.zondervan.com. The "NIV" and "New International
Version" are trademarks registered in the United States Patent and Trademark Office
by Biblica, Inc.™ The author has added italics to Scripture quotations for emphasis.

Library of Congress Control Number 2022944335
ISBN 978-0-8307-8439-4
eISBN 978-0-8307-8440-0

Published in association with the literary agency of WordServe
Literary Group, Ltd., www.wordserveliterary.com.

The Team: Susan McPherson, Jeff Gerke, James Hershberger,
Jack Campbell, Michael Fedison, Susan Murdock
Cover Design: Micah Kandros

Printed in the United States of America
First Edition 2023

1 2 3 4 5 6 7 8 9 10

031523

I would like to dedicate this book to my parents, who so beautifully represented God to me growing up. In the midst of very difficult circumstances, the light of Jesus shined brightly through them. To me, they are true heroes, and I thank God for them.

Acknowledgments

I would like to thank Jeff, Susan, and the David C Cook team for seeing the vision for this book and making it better. I could not have asked for a more gracious and encouraging team.

A big thanks to my assistant, Beth, who has been a tireless voice of encouragement to me and has pored over more revisions and changes than I could count.

Thanks to Greg, who took me on and made this book possible because he believes in its message.

Finally, thanks to the many courageous believers who've inspired me over the years by facing into their stories, hurts, and confusions, to emerge as a beautiful masterpiece of God's grace.

Contents

Acknowledgments   11

Foreword   15

Introduction   17

Chapter 1—Why We Struggle   31

Chapter 2—Designed That Way   43

Chapter 3—God Can't Ultimately Satisfy   69

Chapter 4—An Unattractive Jesus   89

Chapter 5—Why Do I Struggle with the Church?   109

Chapter 6—Where Do I Go in Times of Need?   123

Chapter 7—Why Do I Feel So Wounded by God?   139

Chapter 8—Wait, God Did What?   161

Chapter 9—Afterwards   197

Conclusion   217

Notes   221

Foreword

Count us in the collection of Christ followers who trust God's promises and yet still find themselves feeling like God may not care about them in a pinch. Our self-preserving "do it yourself" attitude can make us question our salvation at times and, even some days, our faith.

As flawed people, we disappoint others and get disappointed when things don't go the way we feel they should go. People who we know love us don't always show up or follow through on their word. Sometimes terrible things just happen to us. Without realizing it, all these experiences can trickle upward to our view of God.

We want intimacy with God but never really learned how to go about doing that. Staying in the Word, understanding the lessons from all the examples of imperfect people in the Bible, shows us that God is the same yesterday, today, and forever. No matter your story or where God placed you, His enormous grace and love for you is never ending.

Bryan's book *God's Not Like That* is fantastic in explaining and bringing all this together to give you an accurate view of God and His love for you. This book is something we'll be reading and recommending more than once.

Dan "Larry the Cable Guy" Whitney
Cara Whitney, author of several books
including *Unbridled Faith*

Introduction

Over four decades, I've had many conversations with people struggling to find the life with Jesus their soul longs for. The specific details in the following story are fictional, but they accurately reflect the kinds of stories I hear regularly.

Mark was working as a CPA for a local firm. Over his lunch hour, he got into a conversation with a work associate. Kirk was a fellow believer. He had been a Christian for several years, yet he struggled in his walk. Kirk didn't know why, but he found himself often doubting God's promises. He lived in fear that one day, in his hour of need, God would not be there for him.

Mark shared with Kirk several familiar passages of Scripture, along with a well-intended mini-sermon. "Kirk, you know God has said He will never leave us or forsake us. He's said nothing can separate us from His love. He's even said we are safe in His hand, and no one can pluck us out of His hand."

"I know all those verses. I've memorized them," Kirk responded, somewhat frustrated. "I know they're true, but I can't stop these feelings. It seems no matter what I do, I still doubt."

Over the next several months, Kirk and Mark met regularly during their lunch hour to talk. They shared Scripture passages. They prayed together. Mark suggested several good books for Kirk to read, which he dutifully did. Kirk was doing better, but he still struggled. He seemed to be doing all the right things to be experiencing joy in his walk with Jesus, but his feelings of doubt and fear wouldn't go away.

One evening, Mark was sharing with his wife, Sheri, his frustration in not being able to help Kirk. "Why is he afraid?" she asked. Mark fumbled around for an answer, then admitted he didn't really know. "There must be some reason why he fears God will let him down," Sheri said. "I would guess if you dig around in his life a little, you'll find a reason. Mark, you have a strong faith because you have a solid view of God. You trust Him because you know He is trustworthy. Even when circumstances don't make sense, you believe He is still good, and you trust Him just the same. The last thing you would ever worry about is God abandoning you or breaking a promise."

"Yes, that's all true," Mark responded thoughtfully.

"Why do you think that comes so easy for you?" Sheri asked. "Do you remember what we talked about several years ago after your dad passed away?"

"You mean all the ways Dad influenced our view of God?"

"Yes. Because of the home you grew up in, you have a very strong view of who God is. Your faith is strong because your view about the object of your faith is strong. You've said it often in our small group: 'Right thinking about God leads to right living.'"

"That's true, I do say that," Mark replied.

"What you learn about God from the Bible, sermons, and books all makes sense to you because your foundational beliefs about God are correct. Mark, have you ever thought about where you'd be today if you had not been raised in a godly home?" Sheri asked. "You take a lot for granted concerning what you believe to be true about God. You think everyone should trust God as easily as you do, but not everyone has had your advantages. Maybe God wants you to use your godly heritage to help others sort out wrong beliefs about God.

"When I talk about something in Kirk's past," she said, "I'm not suggesting we make excuses for his fears. Just the opposite. Find out why he views God the way he does, and then help him correct his messed-up beliefs about God. You and I both know that if he had a correct view of God, he likely wouldn't have those fears and doubts."

Mark was convinced she was on to something. "How'd you get so smart?"

Sheri smiled. "Have you ever thought about why I've had my struggles trusting God like you do? It comes so easy for you. I've always admired that. I never really understood it until your dad died and we all sat around and talked about what we loved about him. I realized that night the profile of your dad was the exact opposite of my father. I had a really messed-up view of God. I realized how much you and your dad had helped me see that God's not like that. My heavenly Father was not at all like my earthly father.

"I know that seems obvious, but it is surprising how deeply seated some of my warped views of God were because of experiences with my dad. It wasn't until I started making a conscious effort to separate my earthly father from my heavenly Father that my faith really began to grow as it should. You have helped me see God in a way I hadn't seen Him before. You and your dad have helped make my faith strong. Maybe that's what Kirk needs too."

Mark had not realized how self-righteous he had become. He was the recipient of a godly heritage that had taught him a right view of God. Based on that view, trust and faith flowed naturally. A right view of God naturally leads to a strong faith. However, a messed-up view of God leads to a crisis of faith. Like Mark's wife, Kirk may need some help sorting out what is true and what is false about God.

Over the next several weeks, Mark learned about the horrors of Kirk's family life. His father had been unfaithful to his mother on several occasions. Kirk remembered the devastation each time his mom had learned of his dad's latest fling. His mom would threaten divorce and his dad would promise it wouldn't happen again, but it did. As Kirk grew older, he begged his dad not to hurt his mom again. His dad would promise, then break that promise, seemingly without the slightest regret. Finally, when Kirk was twelve years old, his dad just left one day and never came back. He hadn't heard from him since.

When Kirk was fourteen, his mom remarried. His stepfather was a decent enough guy but didn't seem to have much interest in Kirk. He had teenagers of his own who attracted most of his attention. Kirk's mom was not a strong person and was easily influenced. Soon, Kirk felt like an outsider in his own family. His mom's attention was given to her new husband and his family. Her fear of not being able to make him happy and having him leave like her first husband caused her to neglect her son, thinking he could look out for himself. By the time he was seventeen, he was more or less on his own.

Kirk had never really thought about it, but those who were supposed to love him most had abandoned him. Disappointment had become a way of life as a child and teenager. He couldn't count all the promises that had been made and broken. Even so, he blamed himself. As an adult, he would find himself wondering whether, if he had done something different—if he had been a better son—maybe his dad wouldn't have left.

Kirk married young. His insecurities from his family life predisposed him to be possessive and controlling with his wife. He feared she would eventually tire of him and look for greener pastures. She assured him that would not be the case, but his controlling increased, and she felt smothered. She eventually couldn't take his suspicions and accusations and divorced him.

More broken promises. Finally, in his own brokenness, Kirk turned to Jesus. Kirk got his "ticket to heaven" but struggled to really know and trust God.

Now that Mark thought about it, it was not hard to see why Kirk struggled to trust God. Deep down, he had learned that to trust was to be disappointed. Promises were no more than good intentions that were rarely kept. Kirk was being asked to believe something about God that he'd never really experienced in any other relationship. How could he know God would not abandon him as others had? If God let him down, there was nowhere else to turn. That would be the ultimate rejection.

It wasn't that Kirk was thinking these things consciously. But deep down, those experiences hindered him from believing what is true about God. Kirk's head and his heart were having trouble getting together.

As soon as Mark began helping Kirk see that he was projecting experiences from his family onto God, he started to make real progress. Over the next several months, Kirk made a serious effort to compare what he knew to be true of God from the Bible with what he had experienced growing up. Little by little, his wrong beliefs about God were corrected, and his faith began to grow. It would not be an easy journey, but Kirk was on the right track, and there was every reason for encouragement.

Family Matters

This story may seem dramatic but it's not unusual. I've had many conversations with people like Kirk over the years. That's why family matters: because of what it teaches us about God.

Perhaps your family wasn't religious so you're thinking that they didn't teach you anything about God. I can assure you that's not true. They taught you a lot more than you may realize. Everyone has a view of God, and much of that view has been impacted by your family of origin.

More is learned of God at home than will ever be learned in a seminary classroom. In a classroom, God is discussed—but at home, God is experienced. Just as a seminary can teach good or bad theology, so correct or faulty teaching about God can be experienced at home.

When we entertain wrong thoughts about God, it shows up in how we live. A warped view of God will lead to a frustrating and disappointing relationship with God. There is nothing more important in our Christian walk than our view of God, and there is no environment more critical to establishing a right view of God than the family.

Why is it so common that people are dissatisfied, frustrated, or even disappointed with their Christian experience? Why do some people read great books, attend wonderful Bible studies, and have terrific churches, and yet they can't seem to trust God? Simply stated, why does it seem like the Christian life works for some and not for others?

If you're among the strugglers, there's a pretty good chance the root problem is a faulty view of God.

There's really no work-around for that. We will struggle until we are able to cultivate a more accurate view of God—it's part of what Jesus meant when He said the truth will set us free. The purpose of this book is to help you identify and correct wrong beliefs about God that came from your family of origin.

> **More is learned of God at home than will ever be learned in a seminary classroom. In a classroom, God is discussed—but at home, God is experienced.**

When referring to your *family of origin* in this book, I mean the environment in which you were raised. I'm not talking about genetics here. This book is for you whether you had a traditional, two-parent family or a single-parent family, whether you were adopted or in a foster home or raised in an orphanage. Everyone was raised somewhere by someone. For the purposes of our discussion in this book, that's what I mean by your family of origin.

Ground Rules

It's important to get started on the right foot. We all make mistakes. Parenting is hard. For most of us, about the time our kids leave home, we feel like we've finally figured a few things out. So often, our children don't really understand this until it's their turn to parent. It's often only then that the challenges and complexities of parenting become evident.

We are walking a difficult tightrope in this book. What we experience growing up does significantly influence our view of God. We can't pretend that's not true. We need to face it. That's what this book is about. But it's also true that our parents were themselves parented in ways that impacted their view of God as well as their own parenting style. They have their own story just as you have yours. This means your story should help you view your parents' story with grace and compassion, just as you would want others to treat you.

Your parents were trying to figure it out, just as you are trying to figure it out. If you expect grace for your story, it seems right that you would extend that same grace to your parents and their story. Life can be hard, and we all struggle and make mistakes.

Think of it this way: If you have a right view of God, it will come out as an attitude of grace, compassion, and forgiveness. If you are determined to hang on to hurts, anger, and unforgiveness, then your view of God is still messed up. That doesn't reflect God at all. One way you can measure progress from reading this book is to watch and see if you become more compassionate and forgiving to your family of origin or if you become more angry and bitter.

In other words, are you cultivating a right view of God or simply viewing yourself as a victim? One leads to life, and one just passes the hurts on to the people around you. Your goal should be that as a result of reading this book, your relationship with your family of origin *improves* because your view of God has become more accurate.

We all have a story, and we were all raised by imperfect people. It may be that the lessons learned at home were positive and have helped you form an accurate view of God. Or perhaps it will be a mix of good and bad theology learned at home. But maybe the lessons learned at home were painful and have caused you to believe things about God that aren't true. You may be pleasantly surprised to learn that *God's Not Like That*.

My Family's Story

Rarely are family stories ideal. Usually, they are full of challenges and messes, joys and sorrows. Good marriages, bad marriages, single parents, no parents, and on it goes. But in the midst of it all, for good or bad, our view of God is shaped, often in ways that we are completely unaware of.

I had the benefit of growing up in a two-parent Christian family. My parents were loving and supportive. However, my family was anything but ideal. I want to begin this book with some of my own story, to both clarify and encourage.

As a boy, my dad displayed unusual promise in music. By the time he was a teenager, he was playing the piano for church services. As a high schooler, he was offered a job as a pianist by Dr. Theodore Epp, the director of Back to the Bible. Dr. Epp was stunned and amused to learn that my dad was still in high school. The job would have to wait.

While attending Wheaton College, my dad began to struggle with eye problems. One morning, he woke up and said it felt like he was looking through a muddy window. The years that followed were difficult. In and out of hospitals. In and out of school.

During this time, my dad began experiencing serious bouts of arthritis. At times, the pain became so intense that continuing in school became unmanageable. He dropped out for a while. When he experienced some relief, he enrolled at the Moody Bible Institute. He eventually graduated and was employed as the music director at the *Back to the Bible* broadcast.

It was there where my dad met my mom. She was not a stranger to suffering either. When she was a very young child, her dad had died suddenly of a heart attack. Her mom went to work to put food on the table. At one point, her mom had a breakdown, which resulted in my mom going to live with relatives for a time. In those days, there was very little help for a single parent. Life was extremely hard for my mom growing up. She learned to take one day at a time—a lesson she would draw upon for a lifetime.

They found each other and were married in 1955. My parents began a family, eventually bearing three kids: my brother, Bruce; myself (the troubled middle child); and our sister, Diane. By the time Diane was born, my dad's health concerns were front and center. His eyes were getting progressively worse, and the arthritis was spreading to his whole body.

The cortisone used to treat Dad's arthritis eventually caused a stomach ulcer, which forced doctors to remove nearly all of his stomach. I don't remember my dad in any other way than confined to a hospital bed in our living room in intense pain. He died in June 1982.

My parents were two of the most courageous people I have known. Against all odds, they were able to rise above their circumstances to fulfill their God-given purpose for our family. What I am today is in large part due to my parents' commitment to model the character of God under extreme circumstances. *God's Not Like That* is a tribute to them and what they taught me about God at home.

Reflecting
on
My Family of Origin

With each chapter in this book, I want to encourage you to consider your family of origin. Whether you are married or single, we all have a family of origin. Everyone was raised somewhere by someone. That family had a significant role in formulating your view of God, whether you realize it or not. Even the most secular, abusive homes cause family members to believe certain things about God. It's also true that many loving and stable families subtly teach things about God that aren't true.

This book is not about how to accomplish the purpose of the family. It's not really a family book at all. It's a struggling-Christian book. It's about assessing your experiences in your family of origin and what those experiences might have taught you about God.

At the end of each chapter, I will provide a few questions to stir your thinking.

Each chapter will close with a journal page inviting you to write out your thoughts and conclusions based on the information in that chapter.

To begin, let's take a closer look at why we struggle.

Journal Entry

Write down what you hope to gain by working your way through *God's Not Like That*.

Chapter 1

Why We Struggle

I love Christians. I've given my adult life to helping people find Jesus and the life He promises. Yes, it is true that you can find Christians who aren't very pleasant and don't represent Jesus well. You can find poor examples in every walk of life. However, my experience has been that most Christians are sincere people who do want to follow Jesus well.

Our churches are filled with discouraged and disappointed Christians. They are not looking to make excuses for bad behavior. They are good people. I care about them deeply. I want them to find the life that eludes them. They have trouble trusting God. They spend far too much time in the dark with their shame and guilt. They feel like they will never measure up for God and often feel like Christian losers. But why? If we truly believe what we say we believe, why do we struggle?

Maybe you identify with this. Your life as a follower of Jesus isn't what you long for it to be. You sincerely try, but you just can't seem to get where you want to go. You're not alone—many feel this way.

There may be many reasons for these difficulties. People are complex, and life can be confusing and complicated. I am not offering a simple formula for all your problems. It's not a one-size-fits-all solution. However, over the years I have learned that very often, when you sort through the mess, there is a foundational problem: people crumble over time because of a messed-up view of God.

Everyone has a view of God. No exception. When your view of God does not align with reality, there will be struggle. To use the words of Jesus, building your life on a faulty view of God is like building your house on the sand. It's going to come crashing down, usually in a storm.

There is always a correlation between what you believe and how you live. How you live reflects what you believe is true. We're not talking about right answers on a Bible quiz or knowing the right things to say at church. We're talking about what you really believe at the deepest level of your being.

It's common for Christians to say they believe one thing but to live in a way that's inconsistent with that belief system. This is why I've concluded that many Christians don't really believe what we say we believe. If we did, our lives would be different.

Again, there may be various reasons for this, but at the core is often a faulty view of God. Think of it this way: If we had an accurate view of God, wouldn't we be compelled to worship, follow, trust, and serve Him? Wouldn't we delight in Him? Wouldn't we generously give to Him of our time and money? Wouldn't the joy of the Lord be evident in our lives, no matter the circumstances? Wouldn't we experience the abundant life Jesus offers? So why don't we?

There is always a correlation between what
you believe and how you live. How you
live reflects what you believe is true.

Our view of God impacts everything we do. We may believe we are sincerely doing the right things for God, but what we don't realize is that our view of Him has skewed our perspective. Take for example Saul of Tarsus. He was highly religious and zealous for the cause of God. He didn't lack heart, but he did lack a right view of God, His grace, and His plan to send a Savior. It was his encounter with Jesus that led Saul to a right view of God and His grace. His corrected view of God led to a significant life change.

Over the years, I've seen a familiar pattern, in which frustrated Christians get excited about the latest church program or spiritual method, only to be disappointed again. It's a bit like repainting the exterior of the house, putting in new windows, and remodeling the kitchen hoping to compensate for the fact that the foundation is bad. It looks good for a while, but the real problem remains.

From Where?

If everyone has a view of God (and they do), where does that view of God come from? This is the critical question. Some would say from the Bible, but is that true? For some, it is. For many, it is not. Can *you* articulate a biblical view of God? Can you open your Bible to support and defend that view? Is the Bible really your primary source of your view of God?

Please understand that this is not a criticism. I don't want these words to sound condemning. I simply want to open your eyes to the likelihood that your view of God may be off in ways you've never considered. Many Christians formulate their view of God more from their life circumstances than from the pages of the Bible. I'm confident this is true—and it is potentially a recipe for a messed-up view of God.

When those life circumstances align with the biblical picture of God, it's powerful for good. But when those circumstances are difficult or hurtful and no corrective from the Bible has been received, that's trouble. In other words, sometimes it doesn't feel like God is good. This is what we're trying to sort out. Did your environment at home accurately reflect the true character of God? What you experienced has to be measured against how the Bible reveals God to us.

When our view of God is formed only through our circumstances, the Bible is *interpreted through* our messed-up view of God. This leads to even more confusion. Our view of God is the lens through which we read the Bible and evaluate our Christian experiences—so if our lens is distorted, we'll end up with an even more warped view of God. Our faulty view of God is reinforced again and again. As long as this is true, there is no chance of obtaining the life your soul desires.

Imagine you hear all kinds of nasty things about your neighbor or coworker. You interpret that person's every word or action through the lens of what you have heard. Each interpretation becomes another brick in the wall that separates you. But what if you find out that what you were told about that person wasn't true? You have unfairly misinterpreted words and actions, because at the core you believed things about that person that simply weren't accurate.

This is often what happens in our Christian lives. We start with a faulty view of God, and then we interpret both the Bible and life circumstances through that lens, until our view of God prohibits the life we seek. What's more, we are often totally unaware that this is happening. We are sincere, we try really hard, and we read and study the Bible, but nothing seems to help. It feels like God is against us and our Christian life is a failure.

God at Home

Where does our view of God originate? There is no question that it is initially formulated in our family. I would suggest it is not possible to leave your family of origin without a basic view of God. In fact, that's one of the primary purposes of the family as designed by God.

Now, I understand that the family you experienced might differ significantly from the family structure God intended. Perhaps you were raised in a blended family, a single-parent family, in foster care, or something else. But then, that's the point: we are trying to measure what you did experience, whatever that looked like, against what God intended. The environment of your upbringing, such as it was, did impact your view of God.

Your family did not have to be religious for this to happen. They may have been wonderful or highly dysfunctional. Perhaps they never went to church or were at the church every time the doors were open. Whatever the case, you learned a lot about God at home.

This is very important to understand. I am not saying God *should* have been learned at home. I am saying that, according to design, and whether we like it or not, God *was* learned at home. The only question is what was learned. What was learned about God could be positive or negative, or some of both. What is not possible is to come away from our family of origin without a view of God.

I want to underscore the idea that no parents are perfect. I love my kids, but I certainly made mistakes with them. Even as we raised our three girls, we learned things along the way and changed how we parented. I think most parents would do lots of things differently if they could do it all again. We have the best of intentions, but parenting is hard, and we don't get a practice round to figure it all out before being given actual children.

This is not an anti-parent book. The goal is to improve your relationship with your parents, not make it worse. A right view of God is evident in our willingness to extend grace and forgiveness. Unforgiveness and anger simply reflect a view of God that is still not correct.

So, what did you experience in your family growing up, and how has that impacted your view of God? So many people are unaware of how much they learned about God at home. Many Christians believe things about God that aren't true without realizing it. Many times, I've seen people genuinely surprised to discover things they never realized they believed about God.

Again, these are sincere Christians. They are not playing games with God or looking to blame their problems on someone else. They are simply Christians who are unaware of what they believe about God and why they believe it. My experience has been that once people discover their misbeliefs, they can correct them relatively quickly. It's a beautiful moment when people realize, much to their relief, that *God's Not Like That.*

Reflecting
on
My Family of Origin

Our Process

The core issue is how to uncover our misbeliefs so we can correct them. That discussion has to start with what we experienced in our family of origin. My desire in this book is not to stir up trouble or blame the family you grew up in for your problems. We are not wanting to dishonor our family of origin. That would be displeasing to God.

However, there is no way around the fact that our foundational view of God was forged at home. We must wrestle with what we learned there.

Sometimes, the lessons are obvious. More frequently, they are subtle and buried in our subconscious thinking. So often, people don't know what they believe and why they believe it. A typical clue that something is messed up is when we experience an odd reaction to something presented from the Bible.

I was once preaching from John 10, where Jesus presents Himself as the Good Shepherd. The image of Jesus as the Good Shepherd isn't something I made up as a preacher— it's how Jesus describes Himself. However, this image really bothered a lady in our congregation. She didn't think Jesus was a good shepherd, so she didn't like that imagery. I asked her what about that image bothered her, but she shrugged it off, saying it just wasn't an image she wanted to use for Jesus.

The truth was, something deep within her was react-ing to that imagery. Something had convinced her that Jesus is not a good shepherd. Why did she think that? There was clearly something in her story that had created a view of Jesus that was messed up. If she believed Jesus was a bad shepherd, it would limit her ability to trust and follow Him.

Over the years, I've noticed that those types of emo-tional reactions often indicate something faulty in our view of God. For you, it may be eye-opening to learn how much of your Christian walk has been impacted by a faulty view of God. You may also be relieved to learn that *God's Not Like That.*

This journey is not easy. It can be very painful. This isn't a book for speed-reading, either. I encourage you to take your time. Process each chapter slowly as you seek to cultivate a right view of God.

How do we do this? What's the process? The only way I know is to present to you a picture of what you should have experienced at home. Remember, no home is perfect. That's not a realistic standard. As we've said, parents make mistakes. But when we know what the Designer of the fam-ily intended, that becomes the standard by which we can measure what we personally experienced at home.

A bank teller learns to recognize counterfeit money by studying the genuine article. That's the idea here: the truth exposes the lie. I can present the truth, but you will need to discern if you've believed a lie about God. It's like a partnership in which we will work together to create a right view of God.

You may be surprised at what you find when you start investigating the origins of your concept of God through this book. You're not likely to discover dramatic revelations in every chapter. More likely, you'll see patterns that will lead to a handful of light-bulb moments. My prayer is that you will come away from this book with a more accurate view of God. This will pave the way for you to make progress to experience the life Jesus wants for you.

One clear measurement of progress will be the cultivation of a heart like Jesus for the people around you. When we play the victim, we become self-centered. Our story becomes *I'm hurt and I want everyone to know that.* A right view of God causes us to view ourselves, our family, and the people around us through a lens of grace and compassion.

It's good to remember that no one has wounded or offended you as deeply as Jesus was wounded and offended in His incarnation. Yet, sinners couldn't get enough of Him because, despite their sin, Jesus met them with a heart of love and compassion. A right view of God should reflect the heart of Jesus to those around us. Let's keep that in mind as we work through this process.

The next chapter is critical. We must understand the biblical purpose of the family. This provides the framework for the chapters that follow. Every person comes away from his or her family of origin with a view of God. Why? Because God designed the family to function that way. Let's take a look.

Journal Entry

Write out your prayer to God, asking Him to give you what you need to work through the material to follow. Ask for wisdom and strength. Include your concerns and fears as well as the desire of your heart to know God more accurately and more deeply.

Chapter 2

Designed That Way

At the foundation of this book is the belief that God had a very specific design and purpose for the family. As I mentioned, I'm not saying you *should* have learned about God at home; I'm saying you *did*. No matter what your family of origin was like, it taught you about God. Why? Because that's how God designed the family. What you learned about God may be very good or pretty messed up. It's a two-edged sword.

This chapter provides the framework upon which the others will hang. It's critical to understand what is supposed to happen at home so you can begin to discern what actually happened at home for you.

Back to the Beginning

The very first words of the Bible are, "In the beginning God created" (Gen. 1:1). That the universe was made by a Creator cannot be proven by science, but the biblical account of creation is also not contrary to science. "By faith we understand that the world has been created by the word of God so that what is seen has not been made out of things that are visible" (Heb. 11:3). Paul states that the evidence for a Creator is so clear that all people who refuse to acknowledge Him are "without excuse" (Rom. 1:20).

This is no small matter. What we believe about our origin lays the foundation for what we believe about the family. If the universe self-created and we are simply a product of natural selection, then "family" can mean whatever we want it to mean. Some would view the family as merely an evolutionary adaptation for the survival of the species.

However, if creation had a Creator, then that's another story. The purpose of this book is not to argue for or against a Creator. My position in this book is simply to accept the Bible as the living and authoritative Word of God. I do absolutely believe the Bible is God's revelation to us and serves as a lamp to our feet and a light to our path today (Ps. 119:105).

Given this starting point, a good way to begin our discussion on the family is to ask what God has to say about it. If God created the family on purpose, what is His design for the family?

We begin our discussion in Genesis:

> Then God said, "Let Us make mankind in Our image, according to Our likeness; and let them rule over the fish of the sea and over the birds of the sky and over the livestock and over all the earth, and over every crawling thing that crawls on the earth." So God created man in His own image, in the image of God He created him; male and female He created them. (Gen. 1:26–27)

When you go through the days of creation, you may notice a pattern in which God created on days one, two, three, four, and five. But when you get to day six, the pattern is interrupted. For the first time, God introduces Himself with plural pronouns: "Let *Us* make mankind in *Our* image." Understanding what this *image* is will be key to understanding the design for family.

Being made in the image of God is what sets humans apart from the rest of creation. To be made in God's image means, among other things, that we have both the ability and the responsibility to represent God on earth. In a limited fashion, we can be like Him. We think, we reason, we live in a way that's distinct from the rest of the animal kingdom. We can choose to obey or disobey. We can choose to give and receive love. We can pursue God or flee from God. We can carry out God's will or do our own thing. We are made to "image God" to the world.

The plural pronouns in these verses ("us" and "our") are a significant clue as to what we must understand the image to be. At the core of this is the understanding that we have been created as relational beings. We were made to be relational because He is relational. In other words, we, as people made in the image of God, are capable of experiencing relationships at a level that sets us apart from the animal kingdom.

With that comes the concept of a will to choose. As humans, we have the ability to think, reason, love, and choose. In order for relationships to be legitimate, we (as adults) have to have some ability to choose, reason, and decide whether we want to enter into such a relationship. This ability to reason and choose is part of what separates us from the rest of creation. This of course also means we can choose to worship God or to seek to be gods ourselves.

With that, then, comes moral responsibility. I'm held responsible for the choices I make. You can read from Genesis to Revelation, and you won't be able to find a single moral command given to the animals, nor can you find any hint of moral responsibility expected of animals. We are uniquely made with the ability to mirror God in the world, and that includes relational ability, volitional will, and moral responsibility.

Genesis 1:27 records three statements that are critical to our discussion. They may sound redundant, but the repetition is intentional. The focal point is the beginning of each statement. This is a Hebrew technique for underscoring something important. In an oral culture such as that of the ancient Hebrews, the text was read *to* the masses, not read *by* the masses. Techniques to make a point were oral rather than written. They didn't have underlining or bold type.

"So God created man in His own image, in the image of God He created him; male and female He created them" (Gen. 1:27).

The three things the Lord has underscored in this passage are:

- God created
- in His image
- male and female

This is our first hint that marriage is to be the context where we are to portray (or *image*) God. Genesis goes on to say: "God blessed them; and God said to them, 'Be fruitful and multiply'" (v. 28a). He tells them to have sex, have children, and multiply. Marriage leads to family, which leads to more families. This is God's intent.

Genesis 1 ends with these words: "And God saw all that He had made, and behold, it was very good. And there was evening and there was morning, the sixth day" (v. 31).

From Big God to Personal God

The next verse we need to look at to understand how God intended the family to reflect Him is Genesis 2:7: "Then the LORD God formed the man of dust from the ground, and breathed into his nostrils the breath of life; and the man became a living person" (that last phrase, "a living person," could be translated *a living soul*).

The best way to interpret Genesis 2 is to understand that it doesn't take place after the events of chapter 1. Rather, chapter 2 goes back and revisits day six of creation, the day that ended with a *very good*.

One way to understand the theological intent of a biblical writer is to notice the strategic use of the names of God. In Genesis 1:1, for example, you have the Hebrew *Elohim*, which is the "big" name of God. It emphasizes His role as the Creator God. Elohim is bigger than all creation. This is the only name of God used in Genesis chapter 1. I think we're supposed to come out of Genesis 1 with this sense that God is so big that He seems unknowable. How could anyone know a God so big?

When we move into Genesis chapter 2, for the first time we're introduced to the name *LORD God*. LORD is in all caps. Anytime you see that, it's always a translation of the Hebrew *Yahweh* (YHWH). Yahweh is the God who is intimate and personal.[1]

He's the God who makes and keeps covenants with His people. The idea of a personal God may have been unique to the Hebrew people and is captured in the name Yahweh. So you move from the big God of chapter 1 to a God who suddenly is very intimate and personal in chapter 2.

Genesis 2:7 states, "The LORD God formed the man of dust from the ground." You have five days in which God is speaking creation into place: the "Let there be …" bits. But when it comes to the creation of man, it's very different. You might say that on day six, the formula changes. The process is different. The big God of Genesis 1 is now very personal and intimate, as reflected in the change of name used for God.

In day six, we have this picture of God rolling up His sleeves and getting down into the dust. There, He begins to shape and form the clay to make Adam. The word *form* there is a word that is also used later in the Bible to describe a potter forming and shaping a piece of clay. Working with clay is a very intimate medium—it's personal and hands-on.[2] You have this sense of God being involved with Adam in a way that He was not involved with the rest of creation. It's breathtaking imagery. The transcendent Creator God has come near to create man in His image.

The text goes on: "The LORD God formed the man of dust from the ground, and breathed into his nostrils the breath of life" (Gen. 2:7). Wow, that's intimate imagery. Uncomfortably intimate. God could have said to Adam, "Breathe." That's essentially how He spoke the rest of creation into existence. But this seems more personal. You have a picture of God putting His mouth on Adam's nostrils and breathing life into him. It would be right to say that what defines life for us as people made in the image of God is that we are filled with the very breath of God. Let that sink in for a moment.

Back to Genesis 2: "The LORD God planted a garden toward the east, in Eden; and there He placed the man whom He had formed" (v. 8). Notice the repetition of the term *formed* from the previous verse, like a potter forms a lump of clay.[3] Adam is the man whom God personally formed in His image.

"Then the LORD God took the man and put him in the Garden of Eden to cultivate it and tend it" (Gen. 2:15).

I would suggest to you that God's grace was demonstrated even before sin entered the picture. He is a God of grace—it's who He is. He extends unearned favor to people simply because it brings Him delight. God created this magnificent garden that He Himself defined as a delight—that's what the word *Eden* means. We might use the word *paradise*.[4] Once He has completed it, He takes Adam, whom He has formed out of the dust of the ground, and places him into the garden paradise. Adam didn't earn a place in the garden; God put him there. Notice the repetition of God putting Adam in the garden in 2:8 and 2:15. It's an act of God's grace.

As we begin to formulate a right view of God, it's good to pause and see that Genesis 2 reminds us of what God has always wanted for people made in His image. Sometimes people look at the pain and suffering and the mess in this world and say, "How can you believe in a loving God when you look at the world and all the suffering?" It's good to remember that this sinful mess wasn't God's plan. This isn't what God wanted.

> ## Adam didn't earn a place in the garden; God put him there.

We—humans formed with a will to choose—chose the way of sin. We turned paradise into chaos, and then we turned around and blamed God. The whole redemption story of the Bible is the saga of what God is willing to do to bring life out of death and get us back to the garden. It's there where we will once again experience what He's always wanted for us. It's a great picture of the heart of God. It's a right view of God. And having a right view of God is essential.

From Very Good to Not Good

> Then the LORD God said, "It is not good for the man to be alone; I will make him a helper suitable for him." (Gen. 2:18)

The beginning of Genesis illustrates a pattern with each day of creation in which God declares that it is good. But on day six, words that had literally never been heard in all of eternity were uttered by God: "It is not good." Remember, chapter 1 ends with day six being *very good*. As readers, we may find ourselves a bit surprised that at one point, partway through day six, God declared it *not good*.

What was not good? That Adam was alone. The text goes on to say that what Adam needed was a helper suitable for him.

Now, some may find the term *helper* rather annoying, as if the wife is the husband's "little helper." But that's not what the term means. It refers to something very powerful. As a matter of fact, it's a Hebrew term that God uses to describe Himself—for example, when God is with Israel in battle (Deut. 33:26). This word carries the idea of an ally or partner.[5]

Adam needed a partner, an ally, to go through life with. The text states that he needed someone who was *suitable for* him. The Hebrew word could be translated as *corresponding to* him,[6] and I think that's a better translation. *Suitable* kind of sounds like someone I could get along with if I had to. Like, yeah, she'll do. But *corresponding* carries more of the flavor of the Hebrew word. God knew Adam needed someone who was also made in the image of God with whom he could share his life. Someone like him.

The text immediately flows into Adam's job of naming the animals. To the reader, this may seem odd. For the first time in all eternity, the words *This is not good* have been uttered. Poor Adam is alone. About the time we are thinking that somebody needs to help the poor guy, the text rather unexpectedly shifts to the naming of the animals.

The point that's being made is that there was no corresponding partner available from the animal kingdom. The process of naming the animals drives that idea home. Adam is uniquely made in the image of God—the animals are not. "But for Adam there was not found a helper suitable for [corresponding to] him" (Gen. 2:20b).

The text is saying that there was no moment when Adam looked at the animals and thought one of them could be his partner. Not the zebra, not the newt, and not even the dog. Adam had the sobering realization that there was no one in the entire garden paradise with whom he could share his life.

So the LORD God caused a deep sleep to fall upon
the man, and he slept; then He took one of his ribs
and closed up the flesh at that place. And the LORD
God fashioned into a woman the rib which He had
taken from the man, and brought her to the man.
Then the man said,

> "At last this is bone of my bones,
> And flesh of my flesh;
> She shall be called 'woman,'
> Because she was taken out of man."

(Gen. 2:21–23)

This is a text that I often use at weddings. Every time I read it,
I find myself somewhat amused. For us as men, we would probably
say that the greatest moment in all of history was when God created
woman. Yet what did Adam do in that moment? He slept through
the whole thing. As a matter of fact, it's even repeated—we're told
twice in verse 21 that Adam slept.

Why does that detail matter? There's a really important theological point being made here: creating Eve for Adam was not Adam's
idea; it was God's idea. Man and woman are God's design. The text
is creatively making it clear this was all God. Adam slept.

Eve Out of Adam

The text says that Eve was taken out of Adam. That fact is mentioned
several times (Gen. 2:21, 22, 23). In Hebrew, even the word *woman*
(*ishah*) reflects the idea that she was taken out of the man (*ish*). This

is a very important detail if we are to understand the purpose of the family.

God intimately formed Adam from the dust of the ground. So why didn't He create Eve the same way? Why not create both of them at the same time? Did God not realize that Adam would need a partner? Did He just forget? Why did God reach in and take a rib out of Adam to create the woman?

I believe there is a message in the fact that man and woman were created at different times and in different ways. Think of it like this: God existed, and out of God came the rest of creation, including people made in His image. Adam existed, and out of Adam came Eve. The woman was made for a relationship with man just as people were made for a relationship with God. One is a picture of the other.

Let's look at what we've learned so far in Genesis. I believe that for all eternity, God was alone. Before there was anything, there was God. However, He wasn't exactly alone. This mysterious doctrine called the Trinity reminds us that through all eternity, God has been a relational being living in intimate relationship with Himself. That's the essence of the Trinity: the Father loves the Son; the Son loves the Spirit; the Spirit loves the Father. That's part of the mysterious wonder of who God is. That's why the name for God used in Genesis 1 (Elohim) is plural.

In the Trinity, I believe we have this beautiful picture of the Father in relationship with the Son, the Son with the Spirit, and the Spirit with the Father. There's this sense in which God is teaching us that life is found not in being selfish, but in loving, and the very essence of loving is being in relationship with another. For all eternity, God the Father has been in relationship with the Son, and the Son with the Spirit, and the Spirit with the Father.

Theologians have referred to this using a Greek word, *perichoresis*. It's a mutual give-and-take that we might call the dance of God. Tim Keller describes it this way: "Each person of the Trinity loves, adores, defers to, and rejoices in the others. That creates a dynamic, pulsating dance of joy and love."[7] As you can perhaps see from the spelling, *perichoresis* is related to the Greek word *choreia*, from which we get our word *choreography*. Forever, God has been dancing in relationship with Himself.

Why did God create anything? Was God lonely or unfulfilled or bored? There was none of that in God. The reason God created is because that's the essence of who God is. It is God's nature to give Himself away lovingly, and creation is simply an expression of that. Creating people in His image was an opportunity for God to give and to love.

In so doing, God desired to invite us, as people made in His image, to give ourselves back to Him—finding life. God doesn't invite us to worship Him because He has a big ego but because that's where we find the life we are searching for. As David states, "In Your presence is fullness of joy; in Your right hand there are pleasures forever" (Ps. 16:11).

Remarkably, God is inviting us to join the dance. We are made with the capacity to know and experience God. The ultimate celebration of the image of God in us is to dance with God.

The picture is unmistakable. The woman came out of man just as we, people made in the image of God, came out of God. The relationship of Adam and Eve is meant to be a picture of the love relationship between God and people. Think of it as actors in a play: Adam plays the part of God, and Eve plays the part of people made in the image of God.

The image is what makes it possible for Adam and Eve to experience relationship in a deeper way than the rest of creation can. Eve was created out of Adam and for Adam. They have been designed to experience intimacy, to dance together. This illustrates the relationship God desires to have with us.

Dance Lessons

Husband and wife are to dance together, not as a substitute for a relationship with God but as a picture—a taste—of the intimacy God wants to experience with them. You might say people were created in the image of God to dance with Him. That's the big dance. But that's not so easy since God is spirit, and we are flesh and blood. What we need are dance lessons. We must learn to dance with a partner to better understand what it means to dance with God. Marriage is a foretaste of the ultimate dance.

It's worth noting that this blueprint was in place before sin entered into the picture. Even in a perfect world, dance lessons were required at home to properly prepare for the ultimate dance with God. Sin and our great rebellion against God had many catastrophic consequences, and one of them is that this process has been made tremendously more difficult.

About now you may be wondering, "So what's the point? What does all this have to do with my view of God?" Well, everything. You were created to dance with God. Your soul wants that. But it requires a right view of God. Where does that right view of

God come from? God intended that He be rightly portrayed at home. Adam and Eve were created to depict that love relationship at home.

But this concept isn't just for Adam and Eve. Genesis 2:24 reads: "For this reason a man shall leave his father and his mother, and be joined to his wife; and they shall become one flesh." What does "for this reason" mean? For what reason? It's one of those statements that would be easy to read over and not notice. "For this reason" refers to what we have just learned about God's intent for male and female.

Now, obviously, Adam and Eve did not have a father and mother, so 2:24 does not refer to them but to the larger picture. The text is referring to marriage and the purpose of the family. A man and a woman will leave their family of origin, and the two of them will be joined to one another, creating a new family. One family gives birth to a new family, which, in turn, gives birth to another new family. This is what it means to be fruitful and multiply (Gen. 1:28).

The word *joined* translates a Hebrew word that means "to glue together." It's a strong word. The KJV translates it as *cleave*.[8] God's intent for people is to leave and cleave. To be fruitful and multiply requires sexual intimacy, which is a beautiful celebration of the image of God in us. In a sense, our sexual drive is our soul's longing to be intimate with God. We get a taste in marriage but find our fulfillment in God.

As this verse clearly shows, sexual intimacy is intended to be in the context of a lifelong, one-flesh, married relationship between man and woman. This is critical to understand if God's design and purpose for the family is going to be obeyed. Two become one—that's God's design. They are to be fruitful and multiply, which takes it from marriage to family.

Contrary to modern thought, marriage and family did not just happen. This system was created and designed by God for a reason. This is why your family of origin has so deeply impacted your view of God.

What Is the Biblical Purpose of the Family?

When we read the Old and New Testaments, we find no specific verses that say, "This is the purpose of the family." I believe the reason for this is that God wants us to see the big picture and how we fit into it. As the Bible unfolds the purpose for the nation of Israel and the mission of the church, we see how the family is found in God's overall purpose.

We have already looked at God's original blueprint for the family from Genesis. God's image is celebrated and experienced as two people, a man and a woman, coming together, becoming one flesh. Marriage and family then become the place where God is portrayed and experienced in real and practical ways.

Children grow up and "leave and cleave," forming a new family unit. This creates a multiplying effect, thus fulfilling God's command to multiply and fill the earth. The idea is not to be fruitful and fill the earth with lots of people; it's to fill the earth with people who love and worship God. The critical piece of this is that what is learned about God at home is passed along to the next generation. To dance with God, I must first learn to dance at home. God's intent is that He be passed on at home.

Teaching of God's Faithfulness at Home

One thing we observe with just a simple read through the rest of Genesis is the emphasis on family. Pretty much everything that happens in Genesis happens in the context of family. Let me offer a few quick examples of this, and then we'll examine your own story more closely.

We track events in Adam's family up through Noah's family and the flood. Next, we are introduced to Abraham as the originator of the family of promise, and then we follow Isaac, Jacob, and Joseph. What we see unfolding is God's plan and purpose being carried out through families.

What is learned about God at home is passed along to the next generation. To dance with God, I must first learn to dance at home.

This continues through the remainder of the Old Testament. Take, for example, the emphasis on family on the night of the first Passover, when all the firstborn of the Egyptians were put to death by the Lord (Ex. 11–12). This was a night of deliverance for those who had wiped the blood of the lamb on the frame of their doors. (This, of course, was symbolic of God's salvation or deliverance from sin that would later come through the shed blood of Jesus, the Lamb of God.)

This was a night to remember. But how? How could children not yet born effectively remember such a significant and glorious night when the people had been set free from the bondage of Egypt?

Exodus 12 explains the plan. It was not Moses' idea but God's, given to Moses to help generations to come remember this night. God commanded Moses and the people of Israel to reenact the events of that fateful night through the Passover celebration every year. Passover was not just a time to talk about what happened; it was also a time to relive the story. The drama would be played out in such a way that the people would taste, touch, smell, and experience the story year after year. Only one generation would live the exodus, but many others would relive it through Passover.

All Israel was to participate, but it was to be done inside their homes as families (Ex. 12:46). Read these words from Exodus and notice the emphasis on children and family:

> And you shall keep this event as an ordinance for you and your children forever. When you enter the land which the LORD will give you, as He has promised, you shall keep this rite. And when your children say to you, "What does this rite mean to you?" then you shall say, "It is a Passover sacrifice to the LORD because He passed over the houses of the sons of Israel in Egypt when He struck the Egyptians, but spared our homes." And the people bowed low and worshiped. (Ex. 12:24–27)

Clearly, God knew that the most effective context to teach His faithfulness was the home. It was in the context of family that God's deliverance would be remembered, experienced, and passed on. For thousands of years, Jewish families have celebrated Passover, reminding themselves of God's faithfulness and their deliverance from bondage.

Notice the emphasis on the importance of teaching children about God at home. When the children ask, you tell them. The obvious intent was to teach each generation of God's faithfulness and deliverance. Those children would grow up and teach their children.

Let's consider another example. Israel, under Joshua, was camped on the banks of the Jordan River, ready to cross and take Jericho. God was going to do a great work that day that would once again demonstrate His faithfulness and power. But how would the generations to come know of God's great miracle at the river? This is not an insignificant question. Future generations would have to fight their own battles. How would they know they could trust God? Read God's plan for teaching future generations of His faithfulness.

> So Joshua called the twelve men whom he had appointed from the sons of Israel, one man from each tribe; and Joshua said to them, "Cross again to the ark of the LORD your God into the middle of the Jordan, and each of you take up a stone on his shoulder, according to the number of the tribes of the sons of Israel. This shall be a sign among you; when your children ask later, saying, 'What do these stones mean to you?' then you shall say to them, 'That the waters of the Jordan were cut off before the ark of the covenant of the LORD; when

it crossed the Jordan, the waters of the Jordan were cut off.' So these stones shall become a memorial to the sons of Israel forever." (Josh. 4:4–7)

The generations to come would know of this miraculous deliverance by asking the meaning of the monument on the banks of the Jordan River. Notice again the special emphasis on how, when the children asked what the stones meant, their parents would tell them of God's faithfulness and power. As each generation discovered the stone monument, it would serve as a platform for parents to teach their children about God and pass their faith in God on from one generation to the next.

Again, it's worth underscoring that the monument was God's plan. These are the discussions He wanted to happen between children and their parents. Each generation would teach the next generation about God. Each generation would have to trust God for their victories. The willingness to trust is cultivated by being taught of God's faithfulness to past generations. God's preferred classroom is the family.

One of the classic Old Testament passages enlightening us on the purpose of the family is found in Deuteronomy 6. Read the passage slowly, listening for the purpose of the family.

Now this is the commandment, the statutes, and the judgments which the LORD your God has commanded me to teach you, so that you may do them in the land where you are going over to take possession of it, so that you, your son, and your grandson will fear the LORD your God, to keep all His statutes and His commandments which I command you, all the days of your life, and that your days may be prolonged. Now Israel, you shall listen and be careful to do them, so that it may go well for you and that you may increase greatly, just as the LORD, the God of your fathers, has promised you, in a land flowing with milk and honey.

Hear, Israel! The LORD is our God, the LORD is one! And you shall love the LORD your God with all your heart and with all your soul and with all your strength. These words, which I am commanding you today, shall be on your heart. And you shall repeat them diligently to your sons and speak of them when you sit in your house, when you walk on the road, when you lie down, and when you get up. You shall also tie them as a sign to your hand, and they shall be as frontlets on your forehead. You shall also write them on the doorposts of your house and on your gates.

Then it shall come about when the LORD your God brings you into the land that He swore to your fathers, to Abraham, Isaac, and Jacob, to give you, great and splendid cities which you did not build, and houses full of all good things which you did not fill, and carved cisterns which you did not carve out, vineyards and olive trees which you did not plant, and you eat and are satisfied, be careful

that you do not forget the LORD who brought you
out of the land of Egypt, out of the house of slavery.
(Deut. 6:1–12)

Again, notice God's desire that faith in Him be passed on
to the next generation. God clearly expresses His concern that a
generation could receive God's blessings but take them for granted.
Each generation needs to be carefully taught so they don't *forget
the Lord.*

How is this remembering to be done? Not primarily through
classes and sermons but through the family—lived out each day as a
way of life. When you sit, when you stand, when you lie down and
rise up, when you walk and talk. It was to be in the DNA of family
life. It was in the water the Israelites drank and the air they breathed.
Notice the emphasis is not on retaining information so as to know
about God. It's about experiencing God, doing life with God, and
knowing Him in a way that is real and personal.

We also have a wonderful New Testament example of how this
plays out in the family: that Timothy was taught by his mother
and grandmother. Paul states, "For I am mindful of the sincere
faith within you, which first dwelled in your grandmother Lois
and your mother Eunice, and I am sure that it is in you as well"
(2 Tim. 1:5).

The Purpose of the Family

Let's put all this together and see if we can arrive at a simple but
profound definition of the purpose of the family. We know that God
intentionally *formed* Adam from the dust of the ground, and that He

then *built* Eve out of Adam. We've learned that marriage is a picture of the relationship God desires to have with people made in His image. We saw that intimacy is experienced in marriage, bringing children into the relationship. This creates a family, the ultimate classroom, where God is learned. For this reason, children grow up and leave and cleave, creating new families—more classrooms. And the process repeats itself again and again.

If we synthesize all those factors, it becomes clear that *God's purpose for the family is to perpetuate the kingdom of God from generation to generation.* In other words, to pass God on. Not just to know about God, but to know Him, love Him, and obey Him—to experience Him.

God has designed the family as the primary classroom where God is learned and experienced. You might say the family is both the classroom and the laboratory where God is made known. This means we learn about God at home, and we pass that view of God on … at home.

It's critical to our discussion to understand that I'm not saying God *should* have been learned at home. I'm saying God *was* learned at home, whether you realize it or not. The question is, "What was learned?"

This has powerful ramifications. Everything at home has something to do with God. According to His design, our foundational beliefs about God are learned at home. This is powerful for good when God is rightly portrayed at home. However, it's powerful for destruction when the picture of God at home is distorted. One thing we know for sure: for good or for bad, God is learned at home.

God's purpose for the family is to perpetuate the kingdom of God from generation to generation.

Whether a home is loving or abusive, godless or spiritual, broken or healthy, it's a classroom where God is taught and learned. No one comes out of their family of origin unaffected by what was learned about God at home. Often, these beliefs are subtle and buried in our subconscious mind. We may be totally unaware of what we learned about God at home. What we do know is that those beliefs will dramatically impact how you live and how you view and relate to God.

Let me remind you that our intent is not to throw your parents under the bus or to dishonor your family in any way. That would be displeasing to God and would lead only to more hurt. The goal is to identify things you may have learned about God at home that aren't true and then correct them so that your life—not to mention your parenting—will be improved.

The evidence of a right view of God will be an outflow of compassion and forgiveness. Anger and bitterness do not reflect the heart of Jesus. They reflect a view of God that is still malformed. My desire for you is that as a result of cultivating a more accurate view of God, there would arise a positive impact on all your relationships. This should serve as a helpful barometer as we work our way through *God's Not Like That*.

Reflecting
on
My Family of Origin

Take some time to reflect on your family of origin. Remember, everyone grew up somewhere and was raised by someone. What emotions are stirred when you think about this? What was that experience like for you? What are the positive words that describe that experience and what are the negative words that come to mind?

What was most important at home? What was celebrated? What were the rules, spoken or unspoken, that defined life at home? What did you love most about your family? What frustrated you?

Overall, was the experience more positive or negative? Why?

At this point, we are just wanting to begin to reflect on life in your family of origin. The chapters that follow will consider very specific areas of focus. For now, we simply want to stir the pot to get things simmering. Pay special attention to your emotions. What are you feeling, and why are you feeling that way?

We can't make progress if you deny your emotions or shut them down. They are threads that lead back to experiences that have impacted your view of God.

Journal Entry

Based on your reflections from this chapter, how might your view of God have been impacted by your family? If God were truly like what you experienced at home, what would He be like? Write your description of Him here.

Can you begin to formulate what you believe to be a corrected view of God? Rewrite the above paragraph by correcting the statements about God that you know to be untrue.

What do you think might have caused some of the family dynamics you experienced growing up? What do you know about your parents' stories? List some of the dynamics in your parents' stories that might have impacted how they raised you. Can you view them with the same compassion and understanding that you might extend to a struggling friend? How can you respond to them the way you desire for others to respond to you?

Chapter 3

God Can't
Ultimately Satisfy

The Wilson family sat in church on Sunday, and they became convicted that they needed to be more involved with the poor and homeless in their city. That afternoon, they brainstormed ideas on what they could do as a family to be more compassionate. They concluded that they would assist the City Mission by opening a soup kitchen one night a week. They sat down with the leaders of the mission and explained their idea. The leaders of the mission were thrilled to have the help and gave the go-ahead to open the Soup Kitchen Ministry.

The Wilson family worked hard to organize details and line up the necessary help. In two months, they were open for business. They got off to a great start. Each Thursday night, they would go home tired but fulfilled. They were averaging between twelve and twenty people eating at their kitchen each week. Their excitement was contagious. Soon, the numbers grew to thirty and forty, and even as high as fifty on one occasion. They were the talk of the mission.

The Wilsons were sure this was exactly what the family had needed to motivate them on to greater compassion toward the needy in the community. Certainly, their children and other volunteers were being dramatically affected by the soup kitchen.

After hearing months of glowing reports and an ever-increasing excitement about the kitchen, the leaders of the mission decided to visit. They were eager to meet the people in need who were attending and to encourage the Wilson family for their commitment and compassion. They even brought video equipment, hoping to cast a vision for others around town to do the same.

The leaders of the mission entered the grade-school cafeteria that was being used as the soup kitchen on Thursday evenings. They spoke with the Wilson family and other volunteers. They encouraged them and thanked them for their dedication and assured them of eternal rewards. They prayed together and waited for the people to show up. Slowly, the room began to fill. The once-quiet cafeteria buzzed with the sounds of hungry customers. It was obvious the group had come to enjoy this time together on Thursday evenings.

At first, the leaders of the mission were excited to see so many new faces. But in time, they grew concerned, as they noticed that the people coming in were nicely dressed, middle-class people from the community. As a matter of fact, they didn't see one person who gave the appearance of being homeless or especially needy.

"Isn't this great?" the Wilsons' teenage daughter said as she took food to a table full of her peers.

"Who are these people?" one of the mission leaders finally asked Mr. Wilson.

"Oh, these people are all from our church," Mr. Wilson replied. "They heard what we were doing and wanted to be a part. They faithfully come and eat with us each week. They all pitch in to cover the cost of the food and take turns helping in the kitchen. Isn't it great? Another full house."

"But what about the homeless and needy?" one of the mission leaders asked. "These people don't really need help. When was the last time you actually fed someone who wouldn't otherwise get a meal?"

"See that guy in the corner over there?" Mrs. Wilson responded. "He's come twice. I think he's having a hard time making ends meet. We haven't actually talked to him—he's kind of smelly, you know—but that's what it looks like to me. Because of how he's dressed and stuff, we ask him to sit over there at that special table."

"You mean that box with an old crate to sit on?"

"Yes, that works nicely for him. I kind of think he's used to such furniture," Mrs. Wilson stated in a self-righteous tone. "Because he doesn't cooperate like the others and bring food or money to help, we ask him to only eat the leftovers. It's not fair to allow him to eat with the others if he isn't going to pitch in."

The mission leaders were appalled. They had never seen such selfishness. These people had become convinced that consuming their blessings themselves was somehow admirable. It didn't dawn on them that they were not even close to accomplishing their original purpose. While the "have nots" went hungry, the "haves" commended themselves for their dedication.

Somewhere along the way, the Wilson family had lost sight of what they had set out to do. They were convinced they were being successful because the seats were filled, when in reality they were accomplishing nothing but satisfying their own consumer-driven needs and feeling good about themselves for doing it.

Have you ever noticed how easy it is to pass off selfishness as virtue?

Consumer Families

The story with the Wilson family is fictional, but the problem the story addresses is all too common today. One barrier to understanding God's purpose for the family is what we might call a consumer mindset. Our culture creates consumer families. In other words, it's family for family's sake. It's not necessary to experience abuse or dysfunction to end up with a messed-up view of God. Consumer families teach us things about God that aren't true.

Don't dismiss this too quickly. With all the emphasis in our churches on family values, it's easy to become a consumer family and believe we're doing the right thing, as the Wilsons demonstrated. We can think we're doing what God wants us to do by being all about the family.

But family for family's sake is not what God intended. What some would define as family values may actually be well-disguised selfishness. A soup kitchen for the already well-to-do, for example.

When kids are raised to believe the universe revolves around them and their needs, they cultivate a certain view of God and what God should do for them. God becomes like a genie in a bottle who should grant their wishes. When that doesn't come to pass, they feel cheated or convinced that God let them down. How do you trust a God that lets you down … again?

> **When kids are raised to believe the universe revolves around them and their needs, they cultivate a certain view of God and what God should do for them.**

It's also common for consumer families to create an environment where looking good is more important than being good. It's more about a show for an audience than a true relationship with Jesus. Your family might have been at church every time the doors were open but for all the wrong reasons. When how we look becomes more important than who we really are, we learn to wear masks. We become more likely to pretend than to be authentic. This is an exhausting way to live.

Jim's Story

The following fictional story accurately reflects many conversations I've had with people over the years.

Jim plops down in a chair, mutters a bit, and then starts pouring out his tale. He says he feels like his whole life is coming unraveled. For years, he's felt like a big hypocrite. He comes to church, puts on his mask, and pretends everything is fine. He may look like your average churchgoer, but inside he feels like a loser Christian.

He's in a men's group but keeps most of his struggles hidden from the others. It's easy to keep the conversations shallow and away from the danger zones. Time after time, he's felt the conviction of the Spirit to deal with his issues, yet they remain buried under layers of shame and guilt. Finally, the impact on his marriage, family, and physical health has become too much. He's finally broken and desperate enough to seek help.

If Jim only knew how many people passing him in the halls of the church felt the same way, he'd realize he's not alone. Many Christians on any given weekend would say they put on a mask when they gather to worship. The fear of being honest and letting people see the real person behind the mask is driven by deep misbeliefs about God. Jim doesn't need to hide. God's not like that. But he doesn't even know what he doesn't know about God. He just knows he's driven to hide behind his mask.

Sin Makes Us Hide

There may be many reasons why people are unwilling to be honest when they gather as the church. Sometimes, it's because the church culture is unsafe, or the people are judgmental or legalistic. But often, the issue is deeper than that. People who wear masks at church often wear masks in most environments. They pretend in public but struggle in private, determined to make sure no one ever sees who they really are.

This is the appeal of social media. People can create and post as the person they wish they were while hiding their real selves in the privacy of their basement. The more "Facebook Jim" takes over, the less likely his mask will ever come off.

Where does this come from? Why are we so afraid to be honest and so determined to hide our real selves? Again, there may be many reasons, but one common contributing factor is what we learned from our family of origin. Christian families are especially vulnerable to this temptation because of the external pressures to come off looking like the ideal family. Sadly, many families inadvertently teach their kids to wear masks in public.

As I've said, a messed-up view of God doesn't require an abusive or dysfunctional home. Because all parents are themselves sinners struggling with their own issues, even good families can communicate to their children values or beliefs that are contrary to the character of God. The problems with some family environments are obvious, but for others the issues are more subtle. Often, we are completely unaware of what we learned about God at home and how much that defines our lives today.

The purpose of the family is to perpetuate the kingdom of God from generation to generation. To pass God on. That's the real metric for measuring success, according to God's intent. Consumer families, however, are more likely to *replace* God than accurately mirror Him.

In the Old Testament, we read the story of Eli and his wicked sons, Hophni and Phinehas. Eli and his sons were priests in Israel, but Eli's sons were wicked and profaned the sacrificial system. Eli had a choice to make: he could honor God by dealing with his wicked boys or allow his sons to continue and thus dishonor God.

He chose to leave his sons as they were. God asked Eli, "Why are you honoring your sons above Me?" Eli had no answer. Listen to God's response to Eli: "Those who honor Me I will honor, and those who despise Me will be insignificant" (1 Sam. 2:29–30).

It is a very serious thing to elevate family to the point where it becomes more important to us than God. That is the sin of idolatry. Jesus Himself said, "The one who loves father or mother more than Me is not worthy of Me; and the one who loves son or daughter more than Me is not worthy of Me" (Matt. 10:37). Consumer families don't illustrate God—they *replace* God as the primary focus. This of course creates a weak and diminished view of God for the household: God must not be that important if He is marginalized at home.

In Genesis 3, Adam and Eve believed they could be their own gods. God offered them paradise, but they believed the lie that life would be better their way. This is the great lie: life will be better with me in charge. When they sinned against the Lord, their relationship with both God and each other fell apart. The first thing they did was hide from God. When God is not first, we idolize what we think will make us happy. That leads to sin, and sin causes us to hide. Wearing masks is one way we hide.

Immediately, Adam and Eve were pointing the finger at one another for their sin. Not long after, Cain, their eldest son, committed the first murder by killing his brother Abel. The first family was quickly in disarray because of sin. Right from the beginning, the temptation was to diminish God and exalt self as the way to happiness.

Think about that. Before there was any peer pressure, before all the busyness and confusion of any human culture existed, Adam and Eve's family was in disarray. Why? It all started with a decision to exalt self over God. This is at the root of a consumer family.

If God is not number one at home, who or what is? This subtly presents to the children the view that God is unimportant, weak, or impotent. He's a God who can't be trusted for the things in life that really matter. The message is clear: something or someone *other than God* is needed to be happy.

Investing Time and Money

It's easy to say that God is first at home. We know the right answer. But is this true? One way to answer this question is to look at two valuable currencies in our culture—time and money. If God is truly first, it will be evident in the use of time and money.

No matter how busy we are, we give time to what we value. When backed against the wall, what wins out: a worship service or a soccer match? Perhaps a family dashes in to catch the early service so they can rush back out to the softball tournament. I recently spoke with a mother who was trying to manage her daughter's volleyball tournament, which was taking place on Easter Sunday. Crazy.

I sympathize with these families. Today, we can try to tune in to church online or catch a recording of the service later, but I think we can acknowledge that such things are not the same as gathering to worship live together. My point is simply to ask, "What do our choices teach our kids about what matters most?" It's worth considering.

It's about priorities and values. We're not talking about some rigid, legalistic standard. It's a simple reality that what we do with our time reflects what we value. We always have time for what we think matters most. Choices reveal priorities. That's all I'm saying.

We cannot avoid the reality that we always have time for what we think is most important. How could our kids see our choices any other way? I've watched this now for decades, and the messaging is very clear. These decisions begin to inform a view of God.

I have to also acknowledge that it's possible to be in church every time the doors are open … but for all the wrong reasons. In that case, we would be—to use Paul's words to the Galatians—attending church only "to make a good showing in the flesh" (6:12). This of course also impacts a child's view of God.

Another way to measure values at home is to examine where the money goes. The consistent teaching of the Bible on money isn't about budgets or debt or money management. The primary teaching in the Bible concerning money is that it is an objective measurement of where your heart is. Jesus said it well: "For where your treasure is, there your heart will be also" (Matt. 6:21). He went on to say, "No one can serve two masters; for either he will hate the one and love the other, or he will be devoted to one and despise the other. You cannot serve God and wealth" (v. 24).

Saying that God is the priority and living for God are two different things. I think we know that it will impact kids dramatically if there's a discrepancy between words and lifestyle. Many kids walk away from God when they leave home. Parents seem baffled as to why. Often, the kids are simply living out the values they were taught at home: namely, that God isn't that important.

> **The primary teaching in the Bible concerning money is that it is an objective measurement of where your heart is.**

You cannot be satisfied in life with anything or anybody unless God is in His rightful place in your heart. There are things in this world that bring momentary satisfaction but will not last. Consumer families keep chasing the pot of gold at the end of the rainbow but never find it. The clear message those families communicate is that God can't ultimately satisfy. That many Christians believe this deep down is indisputable when we watch how they live. Their concept of God is weak and diminished.

The Futility of Life

Solomon experienced this emptiness. He had everything this world had to offer: wealth, pleasure, power, position, and a big family. He had it all. But what he didn't have was anything that satisfied.

> All that my eyes desired, I did not refuse them. I did not restrain my heart from any pleasure, for my heart was pleased because of all my labor; and this was my reward for all my labor. So I considered all my activities which my hands had done and the labor which I had exerted, and behold, all was futility and striving after wind, and there was no benefit under the sun. (Eccl. 2:10–11)

It isn't until the end of the book of Ecclesiastes that Solomon reveals what did finally satisfy: "The conclusion, when everything has been heard, is: fear God and keep His commandments, because this applies to every person" (12:13). In other words, he found that only God satisfies.

It's not that all the things he was involved in were bad. They weren't. Many of the things he was pursuing were good. However, what Solomon was saying was that if God isn't in His proper place in our hearts, nothing else will have its proper meaning. No substitute will do.

The best thing families can do is to love the Lord our God with all our heart, soul, mind, and strength. Solomon also said, "Unless the LORD builds a house, they who build it labor in vain" (Ps. 127:1a).

Life isn't easy. What we get here are moments we treasure, but they are mere glimpses of the world to come. They are teasers reminding us that what our souls long for can be found only in God in the new heaven and earth.

You've likely heard these familiar words:

> There is an appointed time for everything. And
> there is a time for every matter under heaven—
>
> > A time to give birth and a time to die;
> > A time to plant and a time to uproot what is
> >   planted.
> > A time to kill and a time to heal;
> > A time to tear down and a time to build up.
> > A time to weep and a time to laugh;
> > A time to mourn and a time to dance.
> > A time to throw stones and a time to gather
> >   stones;
> > A time to embrace and a time to shun embracing.
> > A time to search and a time to give up as lost;
> > A time to keep and a time to throw away.
> > A time to tear apart and a time to sew together;

A time to be silent and a time to speak.

A time to love and a time to hate;

A time for war and a time for peace. (Eccl. 3:1–8)

This passage is often read at graduations, funerals, and even weddings. However, I believe there is some sarcasm dripping from Solomon's pen as he writes those words. I think he's not seeking to be reflective about the course of life so much as he's rehearsing the futility of life. Time marches on through the seasons—but in the end, who cares? What does it really matter in the end?

Have you ever thought about how time itself is meant to dissatisfy? It does. Time makes us long for something more. Time makes us long for eternity. Time is a thief that steals our moments of pleasure without the slightest regret. No matter how good your marriage is or how special a moment with a child feels, that moment can't last. Time steals it from us. The greatest pleasures we experience in this life are temporary. Kids grow up and move away. Loved ones die. Our bodies age. Time marches relentlessly on, and we can't stop it.

Let me illustrate with a special moment that was burned into my memory years ago. It was a day I spent with my oldest daughter, Ashley. It was December, and she was seven years old. You know what that combination means—excitement! We spent the entire day together in a nearby town Christmas shopping, playing, and having a great time. It was one of those magical days when everything seemed to be perfect.

Part of our day was spent in a game room. Ashley was playing a game where you put your quarter in and alligators pop up through the holes and you hit them with a mallet. Each time one is hit, it says, "Ouch!" She was amused by the game and played it several times. Then she said, "You try it, Daddy!" I did. I used my keen, cat-like reflexes and blazing speed to hit enough alligators that the game shifted to a higher level (keep in mind this was a kids' game, lest you get overly impressed). The alligators began to pop out of the holes at an accelerated pace. I was swinging the mallet like there was no tomorrow. Alligators were fleeing for their reptilian lives, and the whole scene was pure bedlam. At least, that's the way I remember it.

All this struck Ashley as hysterical. She was doubled up laughing so hard she couldn't breathe. She literally rolled on the floor. It was one of those special moments I will remember for a lifetime.

Finally, at the end of this magical day, we loaded everything in the car and headed for home. We had an hour-and-a-half drive, so we put on some Christmas music. The ground was covered with a blanket of fresh snow, and the moon was full. Ashley was surrounded by gifts we had purchased for her mom and sisters, as well as things I had purchased for her.

I remember every detail like it was yesterday. Looking over and seeing her buried in her pile of treasures, sound asleep … it was an angelic moment. I prayed a prayer I knew could never be answered, but my heart cried out anyway. "God," I pleaded, "please don't let this moment end." I didn't want my little girl to grow up. I didn't want to do anything but just hold on to that moment forever. But, alas, I couldn't.

Today, Ashley is a young woman living on her own. All three of my girls have grown up too fast. I savored each moment, but I couldn't stop time from taking my little girls away from me. Time has taken my babies and grown them up to face a difficult world. I used to be able to kiss it and make it all better. Now, I can't. One of my daughters has already buried a child and a husband by age thirty-one. As much as I want to protect my kids from such pain, I can't. Being a dad isn't easy. Time marches on, and I can't stop it. I have the memories, but deep down, I know the clock is ticking and things are changing.

> Have you ever thought about how time itself is meant to dissatisfy? It does. Time makes us long for something more. Time makes us long for eternity.

Time has taken away my son-in-law, granddaughter, mom, dad, grandparents, and some special friends. I know no greater privilege on this earth than to spend time with my best friend and lover, Patti, but I am keenly aware that the clock is ticking relentlessly onward. One day, one of us will lay the other in the grave. I dread that day, but I can't prevent it. Time marches on.

My point is that time makes us long for eternity. I long for moments that last—moments, like the one with Ashley, that will never end. I want those precious hours that Patti and I spend together to be endless.

What I long for is a place where time is no more, at least not in the way we experience it today. I want moments to last forever. There is such a place—the new heaven and earth. It's a place of no more sorrows, disappointments, goodbyes, or partings. It's a place where we'll experience far more than we've ever known in this life, a place where pleasurable moments never end. A place where things from this life are redeemed and made right.

Don't underestimate the words of Solomon's father, David: "You will make known to me the way of life; in Your presence is fullness of joy; in Your right hand there are pleasures forever" (Ps. 16:11). Earthly pleasures give us but a taste of what we can have with God forever. This world can never satisfy. If we ever could become satisfied with the things of this world, we would miss out on that which lasts forever.

Those wonderful moments we experience as families are temporary. They come and they go. We can fill our phone with pictures or take hours of video, but we can't make the moments last. This causes us to long for more. In Jesus, we find what satisfies. In God, we find pleasures forevermore.

If this is truly where we are headed as God's people, if this is what awaits us, then it's imperative that God has first place in our hearts now. Eternal values must be lived out in practical ways in daily living. The kingdom of God must be passed on effectively from generation to generation. We can give no greater gift to our children than an assurance of a better world where we'll be together with Jesus forever. We must not settle for anything less.

God intended for family life to demonstrate the joy and satisfaction that can be found only in Him. We love the Lord our God with all we have because that's where life is found. Family should model this, not replace it.

So many Christians are chasing values that can never satisfy. We don't stop to think about how those values were passed on to us or how that value system diminishes our view of God. We've pushed aside what will satisfy to chase that which only leaves us empty.

Who taught us to live that way? Often, they are the values and beliefs cultivated in our family of origin—from people who learned from *their* families, and from *their* families. Often, these patterns go on for generations until someone steps up and makes significant changes. The notion that God can't satisfy is often passed down in subtle ways we've never considered. We end up with a diminished view of God, so we seek happiness and fulfillment in a hundred other options.

Consumer families pretend a lot. They wear masks and tell everyone things are good, even when things are unraveling at home. Struggles are hidden and sins are never talked about. They visit God on Sundays but marginalize Him the other six days a week. Our busyness reflects our desperation to find something that can satisfy. Eventually, the house built on the sand will fall in the storms of life.

In the garden of Eden, Adam and Eve were convinced that God was not as good as He said He was, and that life would be better if they were in charge. This diminished view of God led to sin, and sin made them hide. Not much has changed.

Reflecting
on
My Family of Origin

What were the values lived out in your family of origin? Where did time and money go? Was God really the source of life at home, or was it primarily pursued in other people or things?

Would you say your family was real and authentic, or did they try to pretend to be something they were not? Are you a mask-wearer? If so, where did you learn that?

Examine your own life. Do you really believe that only God will ultimately satisfy? If you say yes, then it should be evident in how you invest your time and money. Do you really seek first the kingdom of God? If not, why not? Is it possible you have a diminished view of God and believe that real happiness is found elsewhere? Is it possible you were taught that God can't really satisfy?

How can you forgive, get a correct view, and apply it in your life and parenting today?

Journal Entry

Based on this chapter, write a paragraph describing how God was pictured at home.

Is this description true or not? What needs to be corrected?

Write a corrected description that you believe more accurately describes God as you understand Him.

Chapter 4

An Unattractive Jesus

Many people today have issues with the church. We're raising up a generation that wants Jesus (or at least a Jesus of their own making) but not His church. There are lots of reasons for this.

One consideration that's often missed is how the love story between Jesus and His church was acted out at home. Do you think it's merely a coincidence that as more and more young people come from broken and dysfunctional homes, they also want little to do with the church? Speaking more from my years of experience than from science, I'd say that the correlation rings true to me.

To want Jesus but reject His bride is the same as wanting to be my friend but rejecting my wife. That's not going to work. To love Jesus is to love His bride. So why is that such a problem?

Understanding the purpose of the family means we recognize that what is learned about God at home can be either accurate or messed up—or both. What's powerful for good can also be powerful for bad. Done correctly, children leave and cleave with a right view of God and pass that along to their kids. However, done badly, the picture of God gets pretty confusing and even unattractive.

Again, to keep us focused, our goal is not to blame our family for our troubles today but to investigate how that experience may have impacted our view of God. To do this, we must seek to understand what we should have experienced at home growing up, according to God's design. And to do *that,* we must paint a picture of what God intended. Then we can compare that to what you actually experienced—from parents who were themselves possibly the recipients of not-great depictions of God at home.

In this chapter, we'll be talking about the role of the husband in the family. The intent is not to fully explain how to be a good husband today but rather to understand God's design. This is the picture as God intended so He would be accurately revealed at home.

One way to think of the family is as a theatrical production in which God wants to depict several aspects of Himself for the audience. For example, we might say, "Playing the part of Jesus and His love for His bride in tonight's performance is the husband. Playing the part of the bride of Jesus and her response to His love is the wife." Done well, the husband and wife reflect the greatest love story of all time.

When children learn that the relationship between Christ and His church is like the love story they witnessed between Mom and Dad, that may strike them as a good thing or a bad thing, depending on what they witnessed. This makes Christ and His church either appealing or distasteful, depending on how the story was acted out before them.

Sadly, God's purpose for these roles has been lost amidst various arguments and objections. People ignore or object to the idea of roles at home for one reason or another. Sometimes, it's because these roles have been misunderstood and abused at home. We *should* object to that. It creates a warped view of Christ and His church. Other people see those roles as oppressive or unfair or promoting inequality. Certainly, this is true if these roles are abused.

But that's the point. An abuse of roles at home creates a messed-up view of God. Just the mere fact that these roles are so debated or rejected tells us we need to look closely at what we learned about God through our parents' marriage.

It's helpful to recognize that biblical roles are about God, not us. They are not about inequalities or preferences or our rights. They are about God's intent to provide a portrait of Himself at home to the next generation. They are about doing our best to accurately represent God at home so our kids might come to love Jesus and His church. Like parts in a play, both the husband and wife have assigned roles to depict the greatest love story ever.

As a reminder, I am defining family of origin as whoever raised you. You may have come from a single-parent home or been adopted or raised in foster homes. I'm presenting the ideal, what God intended. You have to work through the reality of what home was like for you. For example, you may have to look at the relationship with your birth mom and stepmom. Or maybe there was no father at home so there was no marriage to observe. If what I am describing doesn't fit your situation growing up, remember that that's the point. This is likely where some of your confusion about God originated.

Tradition, Tradition

One common problem is that, over the years, Christians have confused a lot of what might be called traditional roles with biblical roles. Traditional roles tend to squeeze husbands and wives into a pretty tight box. As the culture changes, that box can't change with it. That can be a problem.

When the roles don't fit how God has made us, we should ask why. Would God create a man and woman one way but then require them to fulfill roles inconsistent with how He made them?

God made every person *on* purpose *for* a purpose. In other words, God made you the way you are so you can fulfill your calling. The noblest usage of your talents and skills is to perpetuate His kingdom. Therefore, if the purpose of the family is to perpetuate the kingdom of God from generation to generation, then it would make sense that the gifts and abilities that God has given you should flourish more at home than anywhere else. If you don't have the freedom at home to be who God made you to be, then something at home isn't right.

Please understand: when we talk about the freedom to be you at home, we're not talking about overlooking or excusing bad, selfish, or immature behavior. The freedom to be you means you as God intended; you as God called you to be. Not just you any old way you feel like being.

I'm talking about personality, temperaments, talents, and skills. A man and woman should be able to be themselves at home. So then, for example, what do we do with a woman who is a gifted leader? Should she be expected to stuff that gift at home? If the husband is a mild-mannered, quiet, introspective man, should he have to be something at home that he's not wired to be? What sense does that make, given our understanding of God as the Creator? The home shouldn't be a place where strengths are stuffed, and roles should not force us to operate in the area of our weaknesses.

God made every person *on* purpose *for* a purpose. In other words, God made you the way you are so you can fulfill your calling.

Let me say that if you are thinking traditional roles here rather than biblical roles, this may sound confusing. Traditional roles would say the husband should be the dominant leader at home. But if the man always has to be the strongest personality to lead at home, what do you do with marriages where that's simply not the case? I know many godly women who are dynamic leaders, often more so than their husbands. God made them that way. Now what?

I believe that when biblical roles are rightly understood, the wife is free to be herself within the helper role God has given her. She's free to be herself but not free to take over the marriage. The quieter husband is free to be himself, as well, but he cannot abdicate his role and become passive at home. The roles have been assigned by God, so they do matter.

Think about a business owner who is quiet and thoughtful but not very dynamic. He hires a woman who is a dynamic leader to be his office manager. She is hired to lead effectively, but that doesn't imply she has freedom to take over the company. The owner is still responsible for the company, but he knows how to maximize talent. Done correctly, everyone wins.

It's sad that so many men and women flourish with their talents and skills in the marketplace but experience frustration at home. What a disappointment it must be for God to see what He has given to perpetuate His kingdom used to build earthly empires but stuffed at home.

A key ingredient for a positive experience at home is for the husband and wife to flourish at home in harmony with the way God has made them. Roles should be liberating, not suffocating. Our homes need to be a place of celebration of who we are as people made in God's image.

A Picture of Jesus

The purpose of the family is to perpetuate the kingdom of God from generation to generation. To depict God at home for the next generation. This must include a beautiful and compelling portrait of Jesus and His bride, the church.

Let's begin with the role of the husband. Again, the key is to remember that this is God instructing us about how He wants to be pictured at home. The husband's role is beautifully described by Paul in one of my favorite New Testament letters:

> Husbands, love your wives, just as Christ also loved the church and gave Himself up for her, so that He might sanctify her, having cleansed her by the washing of water with the word, that He might present to Himself the church in all her glory, having no spot or wrinkle or any such thing; but that she would be holy and blameless. So husbands also ought to love their own wives as their own bodies. He who loves his own wife loves himself; for no one ever hated

his own flesh, but nourishes and cherishes it, just as
Christ also does the church. (Eph. 5:25–29)

I read this text at a wedding awhile back and was afterwards
greeted by several younger women who said they'd initially thought,
Oh no, here we go ... They were in panic mode that this text was
being read at a wedding. I know these girls well. They are all about
the age of my daughters and are committed believers. I think in
part they were simply having some fun with me, but I also think
their perspective reveals a wider misunderstanding of biblical roles
in marriage. They went on to say that they appreciated the way I
defined the roles in the wedding message.

According to the text, husbands are to illustrate Christ's selfless
love for His church. The imagery is unmistakable. Jesus so loved His
bride that He humbled Himself to die on a cross to present His bride
"as a radiant church, without stain or wrinkle or any other blemish,
but holy and blameless" (Eph. 5:27 NIV). Husbands are to love their
wives in the same way. Husbands are to emulate the love of Christ
at home.

So, if the husband has the responsibility to depict Christ and to
present his wife before God, then he must also be given the authority
to carry out his responsibility. Imagine being given responsibilities at
work but no authority to carry out those responsibilities. That would
be unfair. Along with God-given responsibility, then, must come the
authority to fulfill that calling.

This authority is called the *headship* role of the husband. "For
the husband is the head of the wife, as Christ also is the head of the

church" (Eph. 5:23). As Christ has authority in the church, so the husband has authority in the home. As the church is submissive to the headship of Christ, so must the wife be in submission to the headship of the husband, since he is the one given the authority to carry out his God-given responsibility.

Sadly, far too many men have taken the idea of the headship role and used it as an excuse to dominate their wives. If you have been exposed to that, you may be having an emotional reaction to what I'm suggesting in this chapter. Please stay with me. The abuse of that role is exactly the point: it is offensive and distorts the picture of who Jesus is as the *head* of the church.

Headship and *leadership* are not synonyms. Headship is more like being the business owner in our previous illustration. He is responsible for the culture and success of the business, but that does not imply he is the strongest natural leader in the company. It does imply that he is *ultimately* responsible for the business.

Secondly, headship does not imply that the man is the king of his castle. Just like in a play, the actor is not actually the character. Just because you play Abraham Lincoln in a play doesn't mean you deserve to have your head on Mount Rushmore. The husband is depicting Jesus at home, but of course he's not actually Jesus.

Headship does not mean he's the boss man. He is portraying Jesus as the head of the church. Headship relates to the responsibility the husband has toward his wife before God. As Jesus did, the husband must die to himself to create an environment where his wife can flourish in the way God made her.

Let's think about this idea of headship as it relates to the larger context of the book of Ephesians. Our introduction to *headship* is not in Ephesians chapter five but in chapter one, in verses 18–23, where Jesus is revealed as the *head* of the church. Jesus' headship is not held up as a negative, of course, but rather as a glorious act of grace toward His church.

Paul is saying that Jesus is awesome, He rules the universe, and everything is under His authority. And in an act of marvelous grace, He chooses to personally be head of His church and fill her with His fullness. What Jesus has done for us as head of the church is unveiled in the first three chapters of Ephesians.

When Paul introduces the husband as head, he has the same glorious grace in mind. There is no reason to think that he has now turned the image into anything negative. Headship is glorious when we learn about it in chapters 1–3, and it's still glorious in chapter 5, when the husband is said to represent Christ in the marriage as head of the wife. If we interpret this idea in light of the whole teaching of Ephesians, it can only be positive.

Roles in Paradise

Marriage roles cannot be dismissed as merely a cultural thing from the first century. Roles of the husband and wife existed before the fall. That means that these roles are not concessions due to the fall. In Genesis 2:23, before sin entered the picture, Adam said, "She shall be called 'woman,'" perhaps meaning *from man,* which was indicative of his role as head. Naming was considered an act of authority. For example, you have authority to name your own child but not the neighbor's child (not to give him his legal name, anyway).

In addition, remember that the method God used to create the woman was different from the one He used to create the man. Adam was formed from the ground, but Eve was fashioned from the man. This is a key ingredient for making our case that marriage is to be a picture of the love relationship between God and people.

Also, we have to remember that Adam and Eve were created at different times. They were not created side by side at the same time in the same way. There must be a reason for that. Adam was created first, then later Eve was created out of Adam. One is not more than or less than the other—just different. There is a reason God created male and female differently. Different time, different way.

Paul makes this argument when he states: "For it was Adam who was first created, and then Eve" (1 Tim. 2:13). He made a similar argument to the Corinthians: "For man does not originate from woman, but woman from man" (1 Cor. 11:8). In other words, these roles—including the man's headship role in marriage—existed as a part of the original creation order, not because of the fall. That makes sense when we realize the purpose of both the family and its roles.

So, the man has authority to fulfill his responsibility, but what *is* his responsibility? According to Ephesians 5, he must provide an environment where his wife (and children) can flourish, especially in her relationship with Christ. He is to illustrate what Christ did for His bride.

How is this done? A husband must die to his selfish desires and serve his family. Isn't that what Jesus did for the church? Of course, Jesus did not have selfish desires, but the text says He gave Himself up to redeem her. In the same way, a husband must give himself up for his wife. He is to love his family as Christ loved the church (Eph. 5:25). Read the first three chapters of Ephesians to learn more of what Jesus did for His bride.

At home, Jesus needs to be not only discussed but also mirrored and experienced. A husband should be able to say to his children when he tucks them in bed at night, "Kids, if you want to know how Jesus loves you, just watch how I love your mom."

Now, it's obvious that none of us are perfect as husbands, and we don't model Jesus rightly all the time. But this is the calling: to rightly demonstrate the love of Christ at home to our spouse and kids. I can't think of a higher calling. We must take this seriously and strive to correctly depict Jesus at home.

God intended for this picture of Christ and His love for His bride to be part of the everyday life of the family. As children grow up, they should observe the selfless love of their dad for their mom. They should see how he serves her and loves her and causes her to flourish. As they continue to grow, they should begin to learn that their dad has been illustrating Christ's love for His church. They will learn that Jesus loves them and wants them to flourish in the way He's made them. That's how the love of Jesus goes from an abstract theological concept to a practical reality: by the children seeing it pictured in daily life.

Husbands may ask, "Okay, but what about *my* needs?" Good question.

> So husbands also ought to love their own wives as their own bodies. He who loves his own wife loves himself; for no one ever hated his own flesh, but nourishes and cherishes it, just as Christ also does the church, because we are parts of His body. For this reason a man shall leave his father and his

mother and be joined to his wife, and the two shall
become one flesh. (Eph. 5:28–31)

Paul says that because two have become one, when a husband loves his wife, he is loving himself. Just as Jesus' love for His church results in His own glory, when a husband presents his wife to Christ, he is presenting himself. They are one. When he creates an environment for her to flourish, he creates an environment where he can flourish as well. Everyone wins!

Husbands, Live with Your Wives

The role of the husband is to create an environment where his wife and children can flourish according to how God has made them. How does he do that? He dies to himself to serve his family. What does this mean? I find Peter helpful in this matter: "You husbands in the same way, live with your wives in an understanding way, as with someone weaker, since she is a woman; and show her honor as a fellow heir of the grace of life, so that your prayers will not be hindered" (1 Pet. 3:7). What does he mean?

To "live with your wife" means "to dwell in intimacy together."[1] The original phrase had sexual overtones to it, but it's not limited to that. What Peter is saying is that the man should work hard to cultivate intimacy in a way that is meaningful to his wife.

The term *understanding* literally means "according to knowledge."[2] In other words, Peter is saying that the man, in order to fulfill his role as husband, must know what his wife needs in order to flourish. For the husband to create an environment where his wife can flourish, he needs to know her intimately. How does she think?

How does she communicate? What are her needs? What is meaningful to her? What are her fears? What does she need to flourish spiritually? What makes her feel safe?

Peter describes the woman as *the weaker partner.* That language can be very unpopular today, but he was simply identifying that, generally speaking, the man is physically stronger than the woman. Sadly, many husbands use this to intimidate and control at home. Certainly, in the first century, where the system so favored the men, husbands could physically take advantage of their wives with no fear of consequences.

Even today, it's not uncommon to find men who intimidate and control their wives simply because they are physically stronger. The wife is treated like a hired hand to fetch this and clean that. It's a horrible misuse of power. How would those same husbands respond if Jesus treated them that way as head of the church? Think about how that picture misrepresents Jesus and His love for His bride.

The role of the husband is to create an environment where his wife and children can flourish according to how God has made them.

Before we leave Peter, let's notice that he ties the husband's prayer life with the treatment of his wife. He says that a man should fulfill his proper role as a husband so that his prayers will not be hindered. Peter is saying that if the husband, representing Christ, is going to mistreat his wife, then Jesus won't listen to his prayers.

God will not tolerate a man abusing his role in the home. Until the husband is willing to change his ways, God will not hear his prayers. God takes this very seriously.

Managing the Home

We've learned that the husband is responsible as the head of the home to create an environment where his wife and children can flourish to be all God created them to be. To do this, he must study his wife and learn what kind of environment she needs. He must daily die to himself as an act of worship to present his wife to God in all her glory. He must portray the love of Christ for His church in his love for his wife. This is a high and holy calling for husbands.

There is one more thing I would like us to examine before we move to the topic of the role of the wife. In 1 Timothy, Paul uses the term *manager* to describe husbands. In referring to the leaders in the church, Paul says they must "manage their own household well" (see 1 Tim. 3:4). What does a manager do?

The King James translates the word *manage* as *rule*. This is a dangerous translation as we understand that term today. Many men have used this as a license to dominate their wives and say they're only obeying the biblical role of the husband. That attitude is clearly a misuse of Paul's intent.

The Greek word behind *manager* (*proistemi*) literally means "to stand before" or "to lead."[3] A good manager understands those he or she leads and serves them accordingly. A poor manager doesn't care about others and uses them for his or her own purposes. Husbands are called to be good managers in the home.

Let's imagine I own a fast-food business in the Midwest. I winter in the South and leave you in charge of my business. When I return, the place is a mess. The outside of the building is trashy, the inside is dirty, and there are very few customers. I go through the books and find we are losing money. Who would I hold accountable? I would come to you as my manager. You might have all kinds of excuses about poor workers, bad attitudes, and uncooperative vendors. But when all is said and done, you would be looking for another job. Why? Because as the manager, you are responsible.

Now imagine I return from the South and the place is humming. The outside is immaculate. The inside is spotless. The place is full of customers, and we're making a healthy profit. While I may see people in various places doing a bang-up job, ultimately, I'm going to give you the credit. Why? Because you're the manager, and a good manager knows how to put the right people in the right places for everyone's benefit. A good manager is a student of people and gets them into roles where they can thrive according to how they're wired.

Some employees or customers may credit other workers with the success. Maybe it's actually a good assistant manager or exceptional crew leaders who have created the success. But as the business owner, I know that the key is not who gets the most attention or who the customers think is running the show. The key is having a manager who puts the right people in the right places.

In the family, the husband must be secure enough to allow his wife to flourish in areas where he is not gifted. Everyone wins when both the husband and wife experience the freedom to flourish to perpetuate the kingdom from generation to generation.

The role of the husband does not require a certain personality type or a certain giftedness. There is no husband who lacks the skills necessary to fulfill his role. All it requires is a humble and obedient heart. Any man can fulfill the biblical role of the husband if he's willing to die to himself to serve his wife and love her as Christ loved the church. There's no need to stuff any husband into a rigid box that forces him to pretend to be something he's not. There's also no excuse for any man not to fulfill his God-given role as husband.

The potential for creating a powerful and attractive depiction of Jesus at home is great. But the risk of passing along an unattractive picture of Jesus is also there. For example, a husband who misrepresents Christ at home presents a distorted image. When a husband fails to love his wife as Christ loved the church, he paints a portrait of Jesus that isn't accurate.

Perhaps he is demanding or controlling or selfish. Maybe he is self-serving or always looks out for his own interests first. Maybe he's unavailable or uncaring. Perhaps he's unkind or too busy or preoccupied with his own selfish pursuits. Maybe he's unfaithful or untrustworthy or abandons the relationship. Perhaps he puts his wife down or devalues her or even abuses her. In such a home, what is the picture of Jesus that is painted?

I realize that families can be messy. Your parents may have divorced or never married, or one or both parents may have passed away. You may have been raised with a stepfather or grandparents, or perhaps you split time between a mom and dad who didn't live together. Again, in this book I am presenting the ideal. But whatever the circumstances were at home, a picture was painted that has impacted your view of God in ways you aren't aware of. You have to examine what was true for you growing up and reflect on what picture of God that experience may have painted for you.

In this book, we want to focus on one picture at a time. In this chapter, we focused on the role of the husband. What is powerful for good when done correctly can be equally powerful for harm when done poorly. How many kids have learned a view of Jesus that is not attractive based on their parents' marriage? This can be so subtle that kids have no idea how much their view of Jesus has been formed by what they experienced at home. They have no idea that *God's Not Like That*.

Summary

Let's summarize what God intended to reveal about Himself through the husband. Like assigning roles in a play, God has called the husband to portray Christ and His sacrificial love for His bride, the church. This picture is to be painted by how he treats his own bride. He does this by creating an environment where she can flourish as the person God created her to be. He is to give himself up for her as Christ gave Himself up in order to love and redeem us. This presents a very attractive view of Jesus to the family.

Reflecting
on
My Family of Origin

I've described what should have been. Now compare that to what you experienced in your family of origin. Take some time to reflect on how your dad treated your mom. Do this, even if your parents were divorced or your dad was absent.

If your dad was painting a picture of Jesus through his role as a husband, is that picture attractive or unattractive to you? In other words, if Jesus treats you the way your dad treated your mom, how attractive is that Jesus to you?

If you did not grow up in a two-parent family, what was your situation? What was missing? For example, a single mom illustrates a bride without a bridegroom. What might that have taught you about Jesus? What did your situation, specifically related to the role of the husband, teach you about Jesus?

Your dad may have been a great husband to your mom ... or not. If he was not, remember, your parents have their own stories that have impacted them. Our goal is not to blame and become bitter. It's to recognize the impact of that experience on your view of God and how that impacts your life today. If you don't want to repeat behaviors that were hurtful to you, what specifically are you doing to make changes?

How will you treat others around you differently? Be specific here.

A right view of Jesus should create a heart of compassion and forgiveness and grace. That's the key to moving on well. Where do you see evidence of this in your life today?

Journal Entry

Write a description of Jesus as He was depicted by your dad, specifically in his role as the husband. How did he model the love of Christ for His bride? Is this Jesus attractive to you or unattractive?

Based on this chapter, write a corrected description of Jesus. Which description do you choose to believe is true? How does Jesus truly love you as part of His bride?

Chapter 5

Why Do I Struggle with the Church?

It's common today for people to say they love Jesus but not His church. Often, when follow-up questions are asked, their reasons are less than convincing. It's a bit like having a bad experience in a restaurant and saying you'll never eat out again. It doesn't really make sense.

Often, the issues are subtle. Someone may have negative emotions associated with the church that seem hard to articulate. It can feel like trying to explain to your friend why you don't want to date his sister. No offense, but you're just not attracted to her.

It's possible that those negative emotions go back to experiences you had at home. If your parents' marriage was not attractive to you, it's highly likely that it has impacted how you view the church. While some may want to quickly dismiss this idea, in my experience, the correlation is pretty strong between those whose parents' marriage was unattractive and those who have issues with the church. It's at least worth considering.

Here Comes the Bride

In the last chapter, we defined the role of the husband. We saw that the husband is to portray the love of Christ for His bride, the church. He is to create an environment where his wife can flourish as the person God created her to be. In this grand drama that plays out at home, the husband is to make Jesus attractive to the rest of the family.

If the husband is to depict the love of Jesus for His bride, the church, then the wife's role is to portray the church's *response* to the love of Jesus. Yes, the Bible does say that the church is called to submit to Christ—and that the wife is called to submit to the husband. Let's talk about that.

I realize that the idea of submission can immediately create negative emotions in some people. Perhaps the previous paragraph sparked a distasteful reaction in you. So often, painful emotions are rooted in negative experiences. Perhaps what you're reacting to is the abuse of power more than the concept of submission. The abuse of power does not paint an attractive picture of Jesus.

The truth is that we all submit in various ways all the time. You can't live in a civil society without submission. There are people who refuse to submit at home because they believe it's devaluing, but those same people may lead in the workplace and expect those under them to submit to them all day long. Isn't that a bit hypocritical? It's helpful as we enter this discussion to acknowledge that submission is expected in some way in almost every environment in our culture. For example, every day, we submit to traffic laws, tax laws, rules at work or school, or business regulations.

The reality is that submission must be a way of life for all of us to function in society.

Let's return to Paul's words in Ephesians. It is interesting to note that the Greek word for *submit* doesn't appear in 5:22. However, it is implied from the verb in 5:21. A more literal translation of the Greek text would read like this: "Subject yourselves to one another in the fear of Christ. *Wives, to your own husbands*, as to the Lord" (Eph. 5:21–22).

If you were to remove verse 21, you wouldn't be able to understand verse 22. What does "Wives, to your own husbands" mean? You have to pull the verb in from verse 21 to make sense of the statement in verse 22. Paul links the two phrases so closely that he shares one verb between them.

Most English translations signal that this is happening behind the scenes in this verse by putting some words in italics (like "Wives, *subject yourselves* to your own husbands"). The italics tell us that the italicized phrase was not in the original Greek. This is an important detail to understand if we are to interpret submission correctly in this text.

Paul makes sure we know that the verse dealing with the submission of a wife to her husband builds on the previous verse, which addresses mutual submission in the church. We in the body of Christ are to submit to one another. This means that since husbands and wives are part of the body of Christ, they are both to submit to others in the church, including one another. You could say the church should be defined as a culture of mutual submission to one another under the headship of Christ.

So it is at home. I submit to my wife's strengths, and she submits to mine. That's how it works in both a marriage and the church. Understanding mutual submission is the starting place for understanding the specific area of submission for the wife.

The truth is that we all submit in various ways all the time. You can't live in a civil society without submission.

So, what is the wife specifically submitting to in marriage? I would say she must be submissive to her husband and his role as defined in the previous chapter. If she is going to play the part of the church in this grand drama at home, she must rightly portray the church as submissive to Christ as the head.

In the church, we each submit to one another according to our callings, roles, and strengths. This doesn't mean there is no authority structure in the church. Even though we submit to one another, there are still elders and pastors with spiritual authority over the others in the church.

My role as a pastor includes an authority that is given by God so I can fulfill my responsibility to shepherd the flock. My authority isn't to be used to boss others around or have them serve my needs. My authority is a tool I must use to fulfill my God-given responsibility. This authority in no way implies any inequality in the church.

In the same way, mutual submission in a marriage doesn't mean there is no authority structure. The husband is given authority to fulfill his responsibility to his wife. Within this authority structure, there is still a mutual submission to one another.

So, if the husband is a picture of Jesus and His sacrificial love for His church, what is the wife a picture of? In Ephesians 5:24 we read, "But as the church is subject to Christ, so also the wives ought to be to their husbands in everything." There you have it. That fills out the picture. The husband demonstrates the selfless love of Christ for His church, while the wife demonstrates the submission of the church to the love of Christ. She represents the bride of Christ in this beautiful love story.

The Greek word for *submission* or *be subject* was a military term that meant "to arrange under."[1] It was used for soldiers aligning themselves under an officer. That must be balanced by the idea that an officer *arranged* his soldiers according to what was best for accomplishing the goal, not what was best for himself. A good officer cannot be self-serving. He must be willing to die for his troops, if necessary. Authority and submission are about order and effectiveness and mission, not power and control.

The wife must accept the fact that her husband, illustrating Christ, is accountable before God for his family. That is a sobering responsibility that requires her cooperation. He cannot succeed without his wife's commitment to be part of the team. But what does that mean?

If the husband's role is to create an environment where she and other family members can flourish, then she must partner with him to help him understand what that environment should be. She must share with him what she needs. A husband and wife should work together to determine strengths and weaknesses. A key ingredient of a wife's role is to submit to her husband's role by helping him understand what she needs in order to flourish before God. In other words, she cooperates with his role because she knows he will be held accountable.

Speaking as a man on behalf of husbands, I must say that women are too complicated for us men to figure out. I guess that's part of the mystery of it all. With all my heart, I want to create an environment where Patti can flourish at home and consequently in life. However, to be honest, that's hard to figure out. As a matter of fact, I'd say it's a moving target. What Patti needs from me today now that we're empty nesters is very different from what she needed from me when our kids were at home.

Bottom line: I need help as a husband. I want to do my job well, and I will be held accountable for it, but I need her to partner with me to help me understand what she needs to flourish. Without her help, I stand no chance of getting it right.

If she wanted to, she could bypass me and do it herself. She could seek to do whatever she thinks is necessary to create an environment that's best for her. However, if she were to choose that route, it would make her more of a *competer* than a completer. Our home would become a place of competition where both parties were keeping score and demanding their way. It's easy to figure out if this is happening. Couples who live this way tend to keep track of who's doing what, and there's always a tension around that conversation.

Submission, then, means cooperation. It's a wife partnering with her husband so he can be successful for her benefit. I don't see anything restrictive or negative about that.

More than that, it's an accurate portrayal of the love story between Christ and His bride, the church. This is a challenging and sobering responsibility. We need to get it right. It will require teamwork between the husband and wife to rightly depict Jesus and His church.

Many languages have a grammatical element known as *voice.* This refers to a form of a verb. English, for example, has two primary voices: active and passive. In active voice, the subject of the verb is doing something: "The man opened the window." In passive voice, the subject of the verb is having something done to it: "The window was opened by the man."

The Greek language has active and passive voice, as well. But Greek also has a third option, called middle voice.[2] (English has this too, but we don't use it much.) In this voice, the person is doing the action to himself.

In the passage we're looking at, the Greek grammar used with regard to a woman's submission is in middle voice. Where active voice means I am doing the action, and passive voice means the action is being done to me, middle voice means I am doing the action to myself.

Submission, therefore, is something a woman must do herself. She must choose to submit. A wise husband knows he can't force his wife to submit any more than she can force him to love her as Christ loves the church.

When she tucks her children in bed at night, a wife should be able to say, "Kids, if you want to know how we are to respond to the love of Jesus, just watch how I respond to your dad." That's the assignment of every wife. A wife who is unwilling to submit herself to her husband in the marriage is teaching her children that it is permissible to rebel against Jesus.

> **Submission, then, means cooperation. It's a wife partnering with her husband so he can be successful for her benefit. I don't see anything restrictive or negative about that.**

Of course, we're talking about the ideal—what God intended. There may be many challenges to making this work, challenges that go beyond the scope of this book. For our purposes, we're looking at how God intended to portray Christ and His church at home.

But What If We Disagree?

You may be thinking, how far does this submission have to go? Good question. Paul anticipates this when he says, "Wives should submit to their husbands in everything" (Eph. 5:24b NIV). Not in most things and not in some things, but in everything. Now, obviously, this doesn't mean things that are immoral or abusive. Just to be crystal clear: I am not advocating physical or emotional abuse.

But submission does include areas of disagreement. There may be times when, having discussed an issue at length, disagreement remains between husband and wife and a decision must be made. Remember the illustration of my fast-food manager in the previous chapter? Ultimately, the manager will be held accountable for the decisions that are made. In the same way, the husband will be held accountable by God for the decisions made in the home. Therefore, as the head, he must own the responsibility to make sure good decisions are made in times of disagreement. But what does that mean?

This is not to say that when there is an impasse, the husband always gets his way. That would be poor management. Rather, a good manager assesses strengths and weaknesses and applies them to the issue at hand. There are times when I know Patti's strengths in a certain area are greater than mine, so I defer to her, even if I still have reservations. There are other times when I feel my strengths better qualify me to make the decision, even if Patti is not in agreement. It is in those moments when perhaps the greatest lessons in humility and submission are taught to our children.

The role of the husband is to be so aware of the strengths and weaknesses in his marriage that he is qualified to make the right call in those rare moments when agreement can't be reached. The husband must be both humble and aware enough to know who is best gifted to speak into an issue of disagreement and to make sure that the opinion of the best-qualified person is what he goes with. If the husband or wife always gets his or her way, something is definitely not right.

Submission is easy when everyone is in agreement. So much so that kids take little notice. But when there is disagreement, then how a wife or husband responds may be remembered for a lifetime.

Now of course this is referring to human marriage. In our relationship with Jesus, in which we are the bride, Jesus is always right, and as His bride, we must always submit to Him. The strengths are always His, and the weaknesses are always ours. Any metaphor will break down if pressed too far. But the point is that God desires to reveal the beautiful love between Christ and His church through a love relationship between a husband and wife.

As we learned in Genesis 2, marriage is about completing, not competing. This requires humility and submission. Paul states that to be like Christ, we should think of others as more important than ourselves and put the interests of others above our own (Phil. 2:3). The need for such Christlike humility is never more evident than when there are disagreements at home.

Before we leave Ephesians, it's worth noting how Paul ends his discussion regarding the roles of the husband and wife: "'For this reason a man shall leave his father and mother and be joined to his wife, and the two shall become one flesh.' This mystery is great; but I am speaking with reference to Christ and the church" (5:31–32).

The first sentence is a quotation of Genesis 2:24. Paul is reminding us that God's intent from the beginning has been to illustrate the love story between Christ and His church through the marriage relationship. Before sin ever entered the world, God's design was for marriage to be a picture of the intimacy God longs to experience with us. Beautiful.

The roles of husband and wife are powerful for good when done correctly. But they are equally powerful for bad when ignored or done poorly. God intended the family to be the ultimate classroom. It should be a place to observe and experience the love story between Christ and His church.

Kids who grow up in a home where their mom and dad love each other and partner with each other are far more likely to be attracted to Christ and His church. The picture presented is attractive. On the other hand, when a marriage is filled with competition, manipulation, and conflict, the picture is unpleasant. Who needs that?

Summary

The wife is to be an illustration of how the church should respond to the love of Christ. Rather than competing with her husband, she chooses to submit and cooperate with him and his role to create a beautiful picture of the love story God is seeking with us. When both the husband and wife fulfill their roles at home, the picture is attractive and winsome.

Remember, this is not some strategy we're creating to teach kids about Jesus. This is how God designed the family to reveal Himself at home. God assigned the roles to the husband and wife to fulfill His purpose at home. This is how God wants Christ and His bride, the church, pictured at home.

What I've presented is the ideal. Now you have to assess what you actually experienced growing up.

Reflecting
on
My Family of Origin

How did your mom picture the church and her response to the love of Christ? Is that picture attractive or disturbing to you?

Reflect on your parents' marriage (if any). Was it one you'd like to emulate? Is the picture attractive? Why or why not?

What emotions are stirred when you think about church? Where do those come from? Is there any correlation between what you feel about church and what you feel when you reflect on your parents' marriage? How did your mom treat your dad?

What words would you use to describe church? What words would you use to describe your mom's relationship with your dad? Is there any correlation between the words on those two lists? For example, why do you think some churches are controlling, manipulative, or bossy? Why do you think some churches are weak, ineffective, or selfish?

Why does the church push your buttons in such a negative way? There must be a reason. It's worth thinking about.

Journal Entry

Write a description of the relationship between Jesus and His church *as pictured by your parents' marriage* (if they were married).

Based on this chapter, write down a corrected description of the relationship between Jesus and His church. How does it compare with the description above? Which description do you believe is true?

As a Christian, when we are talking about a love story between Christ and His church, we're talking about how much Jesus loves you. This is personal—you're part of the bride of Christ. Jesus loves His church: it's His bride. What are some practical things you can do to begin to experience healing and love the bride as Jesus does?

Chapter 6

Where Do I Go in Times of Need?

Life can be very hard. As a pastor, I see this on a weekly basis. My heart breaks because of the pain and suffering that good people endure.

When some believers come to their hour of need, they seem to have an uncanny ability to find refuge in God and experience peace in the midst of the storm. Trusting God seems to be as natural as breathing to them. Yet for so many others, that peace in the storm seems elusive. As hard as they try to trust God, it is anxiety, fear, and despair that seem to rule the day. Rather than God being a place of refuge for them, they feel abandoned by God. He seems to be a million miles away.

Too many turn to unhealthy ways to cope. Alcohol, drugs, pornography, and the list goes on and on. I talk to such people all the time. They are not bad people wanting to rebel against God or bent on self-destruction. They are good people, serious Christians, who just can't seem to find the peace that surpasses all understanding (Phil. 4:7). Why is that?

These things can be very complicated. There could be many reasons why God doesn't seem like a safe place for you in the times of storm. One consideration could have to do with how poorly God was illustrated to you by your mom. Of course, it could also be said that the reason some Christians do find refuge in God in the midst of their storms is because of how well God was pictured to them by their moms.

These portrayals can be very powerful for good … or for bad, depending on what that picture was at home. You may be surprised how severely your most deeply held beliefs about God have been influenced by your experiences at home with your mom and dad.

You might say that God was depicted for you indirectly at home through the husband-wife relationship. You observed how they related to one another, reflecting Christ and His church. All true. But there's another level to the experience you had with your mom and dad, a level that is much more personal. This is about how they treated you directly. Once again, your parents did not have to be obviously abusive or dysfunctional for you to learn things about God that aren't true. It's often more subtle than that.

> We can grow up in homes in which the food finds
> the table, the money finds the college funds, and
> the family even finds the church each Sunday; but
> somehow our hearts remain undiscovered by the
> two people we most need to know us—our parents.[1]

I believe most people's view of God is influenced more by their relationships with their mom and dad than by any other factor, including the Bible. For certain, no one grows up without their view of God being significantly impacted by their mom and dad. Even if a parent is totally absent, things are learned about God from that experience.

There is a seemingly endless list of things you may have experienced with your parents that impact your life today. I want to limit our discussion to what the Bible says you *should* have learned about God from your mother and father.

Let's talk more about the role of the mother.

A Place of Refuge

God wants His children to know Him. Not to just have knowledge *about* Him but to have the experience *of* Him. Another way to think about the role of the mother is to ask what attribute God wants to reveal to children through their mother. A good starting place is Psalm 131:

> LORD, my heart is not proud, nor my eyes
>> arrogant;
> Nor do I involve myself in great matters,
> Or in things too difficult for me.
> I have certainly soothed and quieted my soul;
> Like a weaned child resting against his mother,
> My soul within me is like a weaned child.
> Israel, wait for the LORD
> From this time on and forever.

When life got hard for David, he crawled up into the lap of God and quieted his soul. He used the imagery of a weaned child with his mother. Why a weaned child? Because that child is not there seeking food but refuge. Being there *stills* and *quiets* his soul.

This is one of my favorite images of God. Growing up, I always knew I had a safe place to go. My mom. No matter how bruised and battered I got at school or in the neighborhood, I always knew I had a place of refuge. This gave me the courage I needed. I could risk failure and new challenges knowing there was a safety net for me at home.

As a child, I really needed a place of refuge. I needed somewhere to go for quiet in the storms of life. My mom was that refuge. No matter what happened in life, I believed I had a place to go where everything would be all right. For certain, kids will find a way to cope with the challenges of life, but many of those options are not good. God intended for kids to find refuge in the lap of a caring mother.

I believe most people's view of God is influenced more by their relationships with their mom and dad than by any other factor, including the Bible.

David calls all Israel to hope in God as a child seeks his mother. God wanted the people to learn that He is our place of refuge, our safe place, when life gets hard. We can crawl up in His lap and find comfort. That is a very intimate picture of God. It's something that cannot be fully taught in a formal classroom. A refuge must be experienced to be understood.

As I matured, I came to realize my need for a greater place of refuge. I couldn't continue to crawl up on my mom's lap anymore. I also became aware that my mom couldn't provide what I needed for the bigger storms that were coming my way. That was when it became both necessary and natural for me to go from seeking my mom as a place of refuge to seeking God as my safe place. My mom gave me a taste of what God is like.

"One who dwells in the shelter of the Most High will lodge in the shadow of the Almighty. I will say to the LORD, 'My refuge and my fortress'" (Ps. 91:1–2).

A Faithful God

In Isaiah 49:15, we read, "Can a woman forget her nursing child and have no compassion on the son of her womb? Even these may forget, but I will not forget you."

The strongest human bond we know is the bond between a mother and her baby. God has wired a mother in such a way that her maternal instinct works together with her great love to make her willing to forfeit her own life, if necessary, rather than abandon her little one. When God wanted His people to understand His commitment and faithfulness to them, He used the imagery of a mother. Children learn a lot about service and sacrifice from a nurturing mother.

For many, the home is not a place of safety and nurture. Yesteryear's place of refuge has been replaced by hectic schedules and stressed-out parents. What's lost in that exchange may be immeasurable. Where do children go to seek refuge and security if they don't find it at home? They turn to peers. Gangs. Boyfriends or girlfriends. The internet. Frightening, isn't it?

What's more, if children don't experience home as a place of refuge, how will they experience God as a place of refuge? When the storms hit, maybe they panic or experience high anxiety or run or react in ways that aren't healthy. Far too many turn to alcohol or drugs or other unfortunate ways to escape. If you find yourself doing such things, the reason may be because you've never known a place of refuge with a nurturing mother.

Again, remember that your mother had her own story. Perhaps she herself was never loved or nurtured. Maybe she was abused or mistreated in some way. She may have been doing her best but struggled to even know what to do to raise a child well. Yes, your mom may have failed to nurture you well, and it resulted in wounds, some of them deep wounds. No one is denying that. But let's put our energies into addressing those wounds and how they have impacted your view of God rather than becoming more angry and bitter. For your sake and for the sake of those around you, let's keep the focus on that which will bring about positive growth and change.

It's also worth mentioning that how this nurturing will manifest itself will differ widely depending on the personality and temperament of each mom. For example, what about a mom who is a strong leader? Does that mean she can't be nurturing? There are countless books on leadership today that call for leaders to truly care for (nurture or shepherd) those they lead. Many even use Jesus as the model of such leadership. We can all choose to care for and shepherd those we love. One synonym of nurture is *tend*. We may not think of Peter as nurturing, but Jesus commanded him to tend (nurture) His sheep (John 21:17).

In the New Testament, when Paul was writing to the church in Thessalonica and wanted to communicate how much he cared for them, what imagery did he use? "But we proved to be gentle among you. As a nursing mother tenderly cares for her own children" (1 Thess. 2:7). Paul capitalized on the same metaphor that had been used throughout the Old Testament to reveal God's nurturing side. The mother provides a significant picture of God to her children.

The role of the mother is to nurture her children. When she does, her children feel safe. They learn where to run when the storm clouds roll in. As they mature, they learn that Mom provided merely a glimpse of the ultimate refuge. Like a loving mom, God cares about us and becomes our hiding place through the difficult experiences of life.

A Different Kind of Love

I am not saying that the mother loves her children more than the father does. However, I do believe she loves them differently.

When one of our girls would fall off her bike and skin her knee, she would come into the house crying. If she found me first, I would try everything I could think of to make her feel better. I would fuss over her wound (which doesn't come easily for me), clean her up, dry her tears, put her on my lap. I'd do everything I'd seen Patti do, but somehow it didn't satisfy. Apparently, I lacked the magic.

When I put her down, she would go find Mom for the *real* nurturing. Patti worked whatever magic mothers work, and our daughter would go outside happy. The opposite is not true. If one of the girls came in crying and found Patti first, she received her love and care right there and went back outside. She didn't feel compelled to come find me for additional care. Why is that?

I believe this is more than merely cultural conditioning. This is part of God's design for moms. Scientists have learned that a brain chemical called oxytocin is released in nursing moms to create a bonding effect between mother and child. "The chemical is released when a mother nurses her baby, and it stimulates an instinct for caring and nurturing. It is often called the attachment hormone."[2] I would suggest that the release of oxytocin is evidence that God's intent for a mom is to demonstrate His love for His children.

There is something special about the connection between a mother and her children. A nurturing takes place there that meets a certain need in a child's life. No babysitter, day care worker, or even dad can minister to that child in the same way Mom does. If Dad could be Mom, then one of us would be unnecessary.

Pediatrician Dr. Ross Campbell explains that during World War II, Great Britain developed what they called *safe houses* because they feared the enemy would invade their cities. They wanted to protect their little ones, so they put their infants and children in safe houses in the country to hide them. This was all well and good. But while they had enough adults to feed, clothe, and clean up the kids, they did not have enough help to hold and rock the infants and children. In other words, the children's needs for food and shelter were met, but they were not nurtured.

What happened? According to Dr. Campbell, "most of these children became emotionally disturbed and handicapped. It would have been far better to have kept them with their mothers. The danger of emotional damage was greater than the danger of physical harm."[3]

That is one of many studies that have proven conclusively that children need nurture to do well, even to merely survive.[4] Why? Because God made them that way. That longing in children to be nurtured causes them to bond with their mothers in a special way. That experience with their mothers becomes a taste of the relationship God offers us. Children are drawn to their mothers by God's design to teach them about how God cares for His children.

Touched by a Mother

Touch is an important part of the nurturing process. Again, environments that meet needs such as food, shelter, and safety are not adequate if there is no physical interaction.

> Surprisingly, studies show that most parents touch their children only when necessity demands it, as when helping them dress, undress, or perhaps get into the car. Otherwise, few parents take advantage of this pleasant, effortless way of helping give their children that unconditional love they so desperately need.[5]

Here's something to consider: with all the wonderful new devices and equipment for parents to use with their children, there may be some unintended consequences. Part of the natural function of a parent with a child is to physically interact with them. In other words, to carry them, hug them, entertain them, and hold their hand. Think how many times a day this happens. However, with so many modern conveniences, many of those moments are removed.

For example, if an infant goes from a seat at home that becomes a stroller or a car seat, it's possible that long periods of time can pass without any physical touch. While that's really convenient, it takes a great deal of touching out of the relationship. It's at least worth noting that what's convenient may not necessarily be what's best. The relationship needs to be physical.

Love Your Husband

Along with this is the need for the wife to love her husband. While this may seem rather obvious, it is not unusual for the love of a husband and wife to fade as the children become the focal point of the relationship. This, too, is a mistake. One of the best things a mother can do for her children is to love her husband.

Notice Paul's words in Titus 2:3–4: "Older women likewise are to be reverent in their behavior, not malicious gossips nor enslaved to much wine, teaching what is good, so that they may encourage the young women to love their husbands, to love their children." Observe the emphasis Paul puts on older women teaching younger women to first love their husbands and then their children.

The order in this passage is not insignificant. She needs to love her husband as her first priority. Children need to see a loving relationship modeled. They gain security from seeing how Mom and Dad love each other.

It can be very tempting for a mom to pour her love and energy into her children at the best of times, but even more when things are not going so well in the marriage. More than one marriage has received the final death blow when the mother loses herself in her children and the father loses himself in his work or hobbies. Especially in struggling marriages, there is a need to keep the relationship a priority.

Our God is a place of refuge, a shelter in the time of storm. Do you believe that? I mean, do you *really* believe that? Are you able to crawl up in the lap of God and rest in times of trouble? Do you feel safe in the presence of God? If yes, where did that come from? If no, why is that?

> **Children need to see a loving relationship modeled. They gain security from seeing how Mom and Dad love each other.**

Again, I'm aware of the challenges of single parents or uncooperative spouses. This book is not about how to make all this work but rather to present God's design as a benchmark for examining what you actually experienced in your family of origin.

Summary

When God wanted to reveal His nurturing heart for His children, He consistently used the imagery of a mother. God has hardwired mothers to care for their children in such a way that they give their children a taste of what it means to be nurtured by God. Mom becomes a place of refuge, a safe place. This is the aspect of God that she is responsible to represent at home, according to God's design.

Those children who grow up with such a mom tend to transfer that trust to God relatively easily. However, those who experience a mom who isn't safe, who isn't a place of refuge, tend to struggle to understand how God could be a place of refuge for them in the storms of life.

Reflecting
My Family of Origin
on

How do you react to the storms of life? Do you experience peace? Do you crawl up in God's lap and find refuge there? Or do you cope in other ways, perhaps ways that are more destructive?

Take some time to reflect again on your family of origin. What was the relationship like with your mom? Was she a safe place for you? Was she your comfort in the time of storms? Were you nurtured and comforted as a child?

Did your mom have time for you? Was she controlling or bossy or crabby? Did you always feel like your mom loved you and would be there for you?

If God is like your mom, is that thought comforting or concerning to you? Why?

How would you describe your emotional connection with your mom?

How would you describe your emotional connection with God?

Journal Entry

Write a short description of God as He was depicted by your mom. What, if anything, in that description needs to be corrected to have a proper view of God as He's described in this chapter?

Write a corrected description.

Life can be very hard. We all need a place of refuge. A corrected view of God should open the door to experience God in that way in your time of need. The result of experiencing God as our place of refuge should be a sense of peace and safety. A quiet spirit even in turbulent times. What are some practical things you can do to measure how you are doing in this area?

Your mom has her own story. She may have been doing the best she could, given her own hurts and challenges. To not repeat the pattern, how can you be a safe person to the people around you? Remember, to be a place of refuge for others, you need to experience God as your place of refuge. You can't pass on what you don't know.

Chapter 7

Why Do I Feel So Wounded by God?

I have a friend who is one of the most capable leaders I know. If I could have only a couple of people on a team to change the world, he would make the list. I have been with him in countless environments where he clearly emerges as someone at the top of the class. Yet at times he struggles with deep insecurities that cause him to act in ways that seem odd and out of character. Why is that?

Simply stated, he suffers from a father wound.

Some years ago, I read a fascinating book entitled *Faith of the Fatherless: The Psychology of Atheism*. The author, Paul Vitz, Professor Emeritus of Psychology at New York University, was himself an atheist until his late thirties. In the book, he argues that many of the most familiar historical atheists struggled from one thing in common: deep father wounds.

After examining people like Nietzsche, Hume, Russell, Sartre, Voltaire, and Freud, he concludes, "Looking back at our thirteen major historical rejectors of a personal God, we find a weak, dead or abusive father in every case."[1] Vitz acknowledges that there are other factors in play, but he identifies a *defective father* as a significant contributing factor in a person's conclusion to reject God. Of course, Vitz is not talking about well-meaning dads who make mistakes. What he means by *defective fathers* are those who are abusive, cruel, or absent.

That makes sense. If your experience with your father was painful, then the thought of a heavenly Father could be unbearable. The decision to reject a personal God becomes more emotional than intellectual. I have talked with many atheists and agnostics over the years. While I am sure some arrive at that worldview intellectually, my experience has been consistent with the findings of Vitz. The real issues are far more emotional than intellectual.

Again, we battle that tension of not wanting to throw our parents under the bus but also needing to recognize that some fathers did things that were hurtful. Some were extremely hurtful, devastating even. I don't want to minimize your pain or shrug it off as if it were no big deal. On the other hand, our goal is to cultivate a right view of God, which should bring healing and forgiveness. It's a tightrope, for sure.

Several years ago, I met with a very impressive seventy-year-old woman. She was classy, smart, well spoken, and a delightful member of our congregation. She carried herself with poise and confidence. From the outside, you would conclude she had it all together. Yet almost immediately after she was seated in my office, she began pouring out her heart and crying like a child. She shared her story of growing up with a father who reminded her regularly that she never measured up. She had lived her entire life to gain his approval, but that day never came. At the time of our meeting, her dad had been dead for many years, yet she still longed for him to say he was proud of her.

The power of that moment was sobering. Here was a woman of great maturity and stature, and yet she was still longing to be daddy's little girl.

I wish I could say that that conversation was unusual, but sadly it is not. We call this the father wound, and it is all too common. Of all the things that happen at home that warp a child's view of God, the father wound is probably the most common and the most devastating. A few years ago, one of my girls stated that it was sad to see how many of her friends and peers suffered from deep father wounds.

Perhaps the enemy strategically targets the father because God calls Himself a Father. Our first context to understand what *father* means is the home. For many Christians, therefore, the imagery of God as a father is not a pleasant picture.

Maybe for you, God seems angry, unsafe, or controlling. Maybe it feels like God is never there for you or is always disappointed with you. Maybe you feel like you will never measure up. Maybe you are afraid of God, that He's going to hurt or abuse you in some way. Maybe it feels like you never know when God is going to go off on you without warning.

If you identify with any of these emotions, the question is *why*. Why do you feel that way? Have you ever considered that your view of your heavenly Father may look a lot like your relationship with your earthly dad?

But what if God's not like that at all?

God reveals Himself as a faithful and patient God. He's loving, kind, full of grace and mercy, and slow to anger (Pss. 103:8; 116:5; 145:8). He is a God of forgiveness and love. He cheers you and celebrates you—not because you perform so well for Him but because you're His child. He's everything you could ever want in a father. The question is, do you believe that? If not, why not?

Please don't be too quick to dismiss this. Too often, our way of dealing with these painful wounds is to not deal with them. We brush these hurts aside as if somehow they don't affect us now. As a rule, if you are dismissive of these wounds, it usually indicates that your wounds remain unresolved.

The process of working through the pain is not pleasant. However, it is necessary if you hope to correct your view of God and find the life you long for. You may need help to understand that your heavenly Father and earthly father are not the same, but I promise: you can still have the father your heart has always longed for.

Of course, for some people, Dad beautifully illustrated God at home. If you had a father like that, your view of God is probably accurate and pleasant. For you, the imagery of God as Father is comforting and appealing. When done rightly, it is a thing of beauty. If that's true of you, you are blessed.

Because God is our ultimate Father, everything Dad does contributes to a child's view of God in some way. However, there are also some very specific ways a father paints a picture of God at home.

For example, when God wanted to reveal Himself as a loving disciplinarian, He consistently used the imagery of a father. This is not to say that the father is the only disciplinarian in the home, but that he bears the role of primary disciplinarian. The dad mirrors God as the loving father who needs to teach us and correct us when we drift off the path. God does this not to punish us, but so that we might ultimately flourish.

It is in the area of the father's unique role as the primary disciplinarian where much of the conflict often lies.

Instruction through Discipline

The first chapter of Proverbs contains a summary of what the Bible teaches in regard to the father and mother working together to raise godly children: "Listen, my son, to your father's instruction, and do not ignore your mother's teaching" (Prov. 1:8). Notice the different words used for the roles of the mother and father—*instruction* and *teaching.*

The Hebrew word translated *instruction* means "to instruct through correction or discipline." It carries the idea that correction is a form of instruction. The Hebrew word translated *teaching,* used here with the mother, is *torah*, which we often translate as *law.* It's a reference to what we would naturally think of as teaching or mentoring.[2]

Here, in the first chapter of Proverbs, we see the father instructing through discipline or correction and the mother teaching through a mentoring or nurturing role. This is a consistent biblical portrait of the roles of the mother and father.

In Ephesians 6, we see the same emphasis for the role of the father:

> Children, obey your parents in the Lord, for this
> is right. "Honor your father and mother" (which is
> the first commandment with a promise), "so that it
> may turn out well for you, and that you may live
> long on the earth." Fathers, do not provoke your
> children to anger, but bring them up in the disci-
> pline and instruction of the Lord. (vv. 1–4)

Why does Paul mention provocation? Are fathers the only ones who sometimes provoke their children? I have certainly seen mothers provoking their children to anger. Yet the text is clear that Paul is focusing on fathers not provoking their children. What clue does this give us concerning the role of the father?

The context of the chapter reveals that children are to honor both their parents. But what happens when children don't obey or when they drift off course? As we learned in Proverbs 1:8, it is the father's role to instruct through correction. Correction that is not done properly provokes children to anger or exasperates them. That's a negative outcome, but there is also a positive in this verse. Fathers are not to provoke their children; instead, they are to "bring them up in the discipline and instruction of the Lord" (Eph. 6:4).

The Greek word translated *discipline* refers to correction or reproof. It means "to train by act," with an emphasis on physical discipline. The father is specified in this passage because Dad's primary role is to instruct his children through godly discipline. That has the potential of provoking to anger if not done well.

Ephesians 6:4 also refers to the instruction of the Lord. The word *instruction* is translated from a Greek word that means "to train by word."[3] It stands in contrast with our earlier term, *discipline,* which means more "to train by act." Paul is saying that correction includes both encouragement and reproof, training by words *and* actions.

I believe that for dads (and moms), it's easy to get out of balance. We can end up doing lots of discipline with very little teaching. I've become convinced over the years that oftentimes as parents we are disciplining our kids for things they don't really understand. It was clear to us, so we assume it's clear to them. I finally adopted the practice of teaching, teaching, and teaching until I was absolutely sure my kids were clear on all points of the matter. If they disobeyed after receiving a full understanding, it was a clear act of rebellion, and I would discipline accordingly.

Now, certainly there are times when the mother needs to discipline. However, the primary role of the mother is to nurture, and the father must remember his primary role is to protect his wife's ability to nurture by being the primary disciplinarian. This requires teamwork.

When the mother becomes the primary disciplinarian, it becomes very difficult for her to also be the primary nurturer. The two don't mix well. What typically happens with passive fathers is the mother disciplines and the children go without much nurturing. A lack of nurturing will cause kids to act out, which increases the need for discipline, which only intensifies the problem.

Of course, the result could also be lots of nurturing and no discipline, which is another recipe for trouble.

As we have seen with nurturing and mothers, dads, too, will discipline differently depending on their own personality and temperament. There's no one-size-fits-all way to do this. A quiet, soft-spoken dad can be very effective in his discipline, but his style will look different than the style of a dad who is more outgoing or who has a strong personality.

Now, style is one thing, but a *passive* father is a disobedient father. He is unwilling to step up and accept his role as a dad. That's a heart problem, not a personality issue.

When the roles are neglected, it creates a downward spiral resulting in an irritated father, an exhausted and frustrated mother, and insecure children. All these negative emotions are then projected onto God.

Teamwork Is Essential

Imagine a family traveling down the pathway of life. To stay on the path is to follow Christ. Because the journey is difficult, there is a need for nurture along the way. It's the mother's role to meet that need. When the storms hit, she becomes the safe place.

From time to time, the weather gets foggy, and the kids stray off the path. It's the father's role to go after them and return them to the path. Sometimes, this is done through teaching and encouragement. Other times, there is a need for more aggressive correction as the child veers farther off the path. Sometimes, a wise father can even sense when a child is considering wandering off the path and will respond in a preemptive action. Part of the father's role is to teach his kids how to stay on the path when the fog sets in.

> **The primary role of the mother is to nurture, and the father must remember his primary role is to protect his wife's ability to nurture by being the primary disciplinarian. This requires teamwork.**

Each parent knows what his or her primary responsibility is to get the kids down the pathway. On occasion, the child may get off the path, and Mom will reach out and grab him, or a child may fall and skin her knee in front of Dad, and he will need to nurture her along the way. But their primary roles are understood so they can be about their journey and work as a team. Both roles help illustrate God to the children.

We're talking about the ideal, and often the ideal doesn't exist. Again, the primary focus of this book is not on how to create this environment at home. The focus is on how God intends Himself to be pictured at home according to His design. Now you can compare what you experienced at home and what that experience may have taught you about God.

However, continuing to cultivate a right view of God is a necessary step toward improving your environments now. A right view of Jesus should impact your relationships with your spouse, siblings, friends, and coworkers now. There are always going to be issues with your current relationships if your view of God is messed up. If the water is poisoned at the source, it makes the most sense to address the problem there rather than spending time on all the issues it creates downstream.

A Loving Coach

The writer of Hebrews reminds us that what we experienced with our dad is meant to be a picture of God—specifically, how God teaches and disciplines us. As we go through Hebrews 12, notice your reactions or emotions. It is likely that your emotions are going to reveal whether your experience at home with your dad was good or poor—or maybe a mixture of both.

The context of Hebrews 12 is important. Hebrews 11 is a record of the great heroes of faith. These were men and women who put it all on the line for the sake of God's kingdom. Hebrews 11 is often referred to as the *faith hall of fame*. So, call to mind the great heroes of faith in the Bible. Now you're ready for our text.

Chapter 12 opens with the imagery of a relay race. The heroes of chapter 11 had run their leg of the race and are now seated in the bleachers of heaven watching each new generation pass the baton. "Therefore, since we also have such a great cloud of witnesses surrounding us, let's rid ourselves of every obstacle and the sin which so easily entangles us, and let's run with endurance the race that is set before us" (12:1). That's an impressive crowd we have as teammates. They are not spectators; they are members of the relay team, and now it's our turn to carry the baton for the team. We're all in this together.

The problem was that the Christians to whom the book of Hebrews was written were not running a very good race. A good runner needs to stay on the designated course to win the race. Some of these runners had received the baton but were drifting off course. Therefore, for everyone's sake, it was necessary to correct those who had strayed to get them back on course.

This is the picture of a loving coach trying to help the athletes run their best race so that everyone will win. This is not the picture of an angry father yelling at his kids, nor is it a picture of a passive, uninvolved dad. Again, it is worth noting that when God wanted to reveal this aspect of His character, He specifically used the picture of a father.

In these next verses, pay close attention to the emphasis on how the father is a representation of God to His children in His discipline:

> You have not yet resisted to the point of shedding blood in your striving against sin; and you have forgotten the exhortation which is addressed to you as sons, "My son, do not regard lightly the discipline of the Lord, nor faint when you are punished by Him; for whom the Lord loves He disciplines, and He punishes every son whom he accepts." It is for discipline that you endure; God deals with you as with sons; for what son is there whom his father does not discipline? But if you are without discipline, of which all have become partakers, then you are illegitimate children and not sons. Furthermore, we had earthly fathers to discipline us, and we respected them; shall we not much more be subject to the Father of spirits, and live? For they disciplined us for a short time as seemed best to them, but He disciplines us for our good, so that we may share His holiness. For the

moment, all discipline seems not to be pleasant,
but painful; yet to those who have been trained
by it, afterward it yields the peaceful fruit of righ-
teousness. (vv. 4–11)

The comparison is unmistakable. How a father disciplines his
children should teach them about the loving discipline of their heavenly Father. Discipline is an opportunity to teach children about
God. Poor (or nonexistent) discipline gives children a warped view
of God. Good discipline teaches children life-bringing truths about
God. Either way, something is being learned about God.

For example, a father certainly can intimidate his children into
submission. They may act like obedient little robots, which may
impress some. However, those children will likely grow up to be
resentful and to believe things about God that aren't true. Is that
how God disciplines us? Is God a bully? If Dad is unpredictable and
sometimes blows up on the kids, it will make it very difficult for
them to relax in his presence. To them, Dad feels unsafe. Therefore,
God feels unsafe too.

Why do some Christians fear that on any given day God is
going to whack them? Why do difficult experiences always feel
like punishment for some past sin? Typically, we are not conscious
of these thoughts about God. They are buried deep within. All
you know is that you are never able to rest or feel safe in God's
presence.

Think of it this way: if you squirm or feel unsafe in the presence
of God, chances are good that you felt the same way in the presence

of your earthly father. You can't be intimate with someone unsafe. You may fear God's correction.

Conversely, a passive or uninvolved dad teaches kids to *devalue* correction. What's worse, the father who doesn't discipline at all teaches the children to ignore God's warnings and corrections. The kids grow up having no respect for authority. Any correction—by God or a person—is viewed as unfair. Since they have not been properly disciplined growing up, when God's discipline comes, they may become resentful, angry, and confused.

There is an idea going around that says, since God is a God of love, He lovingly approves of everything I do. But that is a myth. If God loves you, He corrects you (Prov. 3:12). And this is a lesson you should have learned at home. There are kids growing up today who are unprepared to face real life. The least little struggle feels unfair and abusive to them. They think God is mean and uncaring as soon as they're faced with the consequences of their bad choices.

Many today seem unable to connect the dots between choices and behaviors ... and consequences that are not so pleasant. The ramifications of not being properly disciplined as children can affect us for a lifetime.

Love and Respect

Hebrews 12 reminds us that discipline is a sign of love. The writer goes so far as to say that a lack of discipline communicates a lack of love. If there is no discipline, he says, you are *illegitimate children*. Those are strong words. Good discipline is not unfair—it is the mark of a loving father.

Perhaps you have wondered why the wicked seem to prosper while the righteous get caught. It may be because the righteous have a loving Father who cares too much to ignore destructive behavior by His kids.

Sometimes, dads avoid disciplining their children because they want to be the pal instead of the parent. The problem is not that these dads love their children too much—the problem is they love their children too little. These are selfish dads who avoid the discomfort of necessary discipline. Discipline is a proof of love.

Discipline leads to respect. "Furthermore, we had earthly fathers to discipline us, and we respected them" (v. 9). Growing up, there was no one I respected more than my dad. Not because he did something great, but because of who he was to me. He was my dad. He was a man of love and integrity. He could always be trusted. I knew, even when I disagreed with him, that he always had my best interests in mind. I never doubted that.

My dad was the primary disciplinarian in our house, even though he was physically incapacitated. He disciplined us through his character and love. Physically, he was not able to spank us, but that was irrelevant. He was the head of our home, and none of us doubted that. Too often, physical discipline is a cheap substitute for respect, anyway. The most effective instrument for discipline is not a paddle; it's respect.

Over the years, there have certainly been times when I've drifted off track in my spiritual walk. God, as a loving heavenly daddy, has gently corrected me to get me back on the right path. When I think of God's discipline, I can't help but think of how my dad disciplined me. I see God, His eyes filled with love and concern for me, doing what is necessary to correct me and get me back on the path. I respect the discipline of God because I learned to respect my dad's discipline. I am absolutely certain that God has my best in mind.

If God loves you, He corrects you.

Children need boundaries. They need to know that there is someone who will correct them when they get off the path. Today, I don't see God's commands as burdensome or restrictive but as signposts that direct me down the path of life. I know God isn't going to stand by and watch me self-destruct. He loves me too much for that. I feel a sense of security knowing that if I stray, God will correct me and encourage me back to the right path. He defines my boundaries, and this sets me free to live with confidence.

About a half mile from my house, there is a set of train tracks. Are those tracks restrictive or liberating? I suppose that on one hand, they are restrictive. The train must stay on the tracks and not wander about the countryside. However, to a higher degree, the tracks are liberating. The reality is that the train isn't going anywhere if it jumps the tracks. It's the tracks that set the train free to glide across the country. So it is with the commands of God. Do they restrict? Yes, in a sense, they do. But they are also the tracks that set you free to experience the life your soul longs for.

If you experienced poor discipline or a lack of discipline, you will have to sort out the differences between your earthly father and your heavenly Father. You may believe some things about God that are not true.

God disciplines you only for your ultimate good. Again, measure your response to that last statement. Do you believe it, or do you find yourself reacting negatively to it? Why?

When fathers abuse their authority in the home, the scars can last a lifetime. Not only does a child become angry at home, but often he or she will also project that anger onto God. I have had countless conversations with young men and women who have been confused and devastated by a father who pretended to be *Super-Christian* in public but was something far different in the privacy of their home. The common denominator in all those conversations was that the father wound became a significant barrier to an intimate relationship with God.

The father wound is real and powerful. Does the concept of God as our heavenly Father comfort you or stir up negative emotions? If it stirs up negative emotions, you have work to do. The good news is that you can indeed have the kind of father relationship with God that you've always dreamed of.

Summary

Fathers represent God in the home in many ways. Anything related to our earthly father tends to get projected onto our heavenly Father. Specifically, fathers are called to paint a picture at home of God as a patient and loving disciplinarian. Not as harsh and angry. Not as disconnected and apathetic. Fathers are to lovingly coach their children along the path of life through encouragement and correction.

If this is done correctly, the child learns that the father always acts out of the best interests of the child, causing the child to learn to trust him and accept correction. Proper correction reveals the love and commitment of a father to his children. Done correctly, the child feels loved, valued, and secure at home. Done poorly, the father wound often leads to rebellion with the children that will hinder any kind of a meaningful relationship with the heavenly Father.

I understand that some of these wounds run very deep. As a pastor, I have heard countless stories of father wounds that break my heart. No one is minimizing that pain. The hope is that some of the damage done can be corrected by cultivating a more accurate view of God. This corrected view of God should bring healing to both past and current relationships and put you in the right position to pass along a right view of God to others. What a tragedy it would be if you passed along the same distorted view of God that so wounded you.

The heart of Jesus is a heart of compassion, mercy, and forgiveness. If that weren't the case, none of us would stand any chance of hope or forgiveness. A right view of Jesus will show up in you as a heart that leans toward compassion, mercy, and forgiveness, as well. Do I want you to heal? Absolutely. Do I want you to be more loving and forgiving to others around you today? Yes, for sure. I want your story to be a good one both for you and for the people around you.

Keep in mind that offering forgiveness is not the same as restoration or reconciliation. You can choose to forgive, regardless of the attitude or behavior of those who have wounded you. But to restore and reconcile a relationship, it takes work from both sides.

It would be sad to avoid doing the work of forgiveness because you have the wrong idea about it—if you resisted it because you think, for example, that forgiveness means acting like everything is fine and sweeping all hurts under the carpet. That would be unwise.

You can forgive. That's a choice that reflects the heart of Jesus toward you. Whether or not you can experience reconciliation or some level of restoration depends on what has transpired not only in your heart but also in the heart of the one who wounded you. I would recommend you talk with a counselor, pastor, or trusted friend before you attempt that step.

Reflecting on
My Family of Origin

Take some time to carefully process the emotions that may have been stirred up in this chapter. Try to process not only what you feel but why you feel those emotions. The clearer you are about what you experienced at home with your earthly father, the better equipped you are to separate your earthly father from your heavenly Father.

Perhaps the emotions related to your dad are very positive. They are good emotions that cause you to view God in a positive light. That's a reason to celebrate. Perhaps this chapter stirs up negative, unpleasant emotions. Take a moment and assess what you are thinking and feeling right now.

It may even be some of both—things you celebrate and things that were hurtful. Remember, our goal is to formulate a right view of God, not to disrespect your parents or blame them for your life today. But a right view of God often requires hard and difficult work, which may include correcting things we learned about God that aren't true.

It's been my experience that wounded people sometimes turn around and wound other people. That's not what we want. We can't change the past, but we can decide what we do with it. The key to not passing our hurt along to others is to determine what we are going to do with our disappointments and wounds. To blame and get bitter assures we are likely to pass the hurt on to others. A right view of God cultivates a heart of compassion and mercy.

"But God demonstrates His own love toward us, in that while we were still sinners, Christ died for us" (Rom. 5:8). If that's how Christ loved you as a sinner, how should a right view of Jesus be manifested in how you treat those around you, including those who have wounded you?

Journal Entry

Write down a description of God as He was depicted by your dad at home. If God is like my dad, that means He is ...

Now compare that description of God with how He was described in this chapter. Which picture of God do you choose to believe is correct?

Based on the corrected view of God you've written above, what are some very practical ways to reveal that God to those around you? How do your words and actions accurately reveal the heart of the Jesus that lives in you?

Chapter 8

Wait, God Did What?

When Jesus walked on this earth, sinners, misfits, and losers found Him irresistible. As a result, the religious leaders grumbled, saying, "This man receives sinners and eats with them" (see Luke 15:1–2).

In response, Jesus told them this story:

> And He said, "A man had two sons. The younger of them said to his father, 'Father, give me the share of the estate that is coming to me.' And so he divided his wealth between them. And not many days later, the younger son gathered everything together and went on a journey to a distant country, and there he squandered his estate in wild living. Now when he had spent everything, a severe famine occurred in that country, and he began doing without. So he went and hired himself out to one of the citizens of that country, and he sent him into his fields to feed pigs. And he longed to have his fill of the carob pods that the pigs were eating, and no one was giving him anything." (Luke 15:11–16)

The young son wanted his inheritance. His older brother, as firstborn, would get two-thirds, and the younger son would get one-third. He gets his estate, and he takes it to another country.

Jesus goes out of His way in this story to make the younger son's behavior as offensive as it could possibly be. The son leaves the Promised Land and dwells among the Gentiles. That alone would have been offensive to Jesus' audience. The young man doesn't just lose his money—he squanders it … with loose living. Jesus drives home the point by telling us that he spent *everything*. Next came a famine, and he went and hired himself out. He became a servant to a Gentile, feeding the man's unclean pigs to survive.

Everything about this story would have been troublesome to a Jewish audience. For us, though, it might be easy to miss how offensive this would've been to the religious leaders with whom Jesus was talking. The story continues:

> But when he came to his senses, he said, "How many of my father's hired laborers have more than enough bread, but I am dying here from hunger! I will set out and go to my father, and will say to him, 'Father, I have sinned against heaven, and in your sight; I am no longer worthy to be called your son; treat me as one of your hired laborers.'" (Luke 15:17–19)

The son's response clearly shows there was a level of brokenness. He finally hit bottom and realized something had to change. There was evidence of repentance and true confession. He determined to go back, even though he had forfeited his rights as a son (not to mention his inheritance), and beg to be one of his father's employees, because that way he would still be living better than he currently was.

I am guessing that the Jewish religious leaders in the audience were nodding in agreement. What the son was suggesting would be appropriate. If the father were to agree with the son's plan to become his employee, that would actually be extremely gracious of him. This probably was a fair arrangement, given the son's wasteful and foolish behavior.

But the story wasn't about fairness. It was about grace.

> So he set out and came to his father. But when he was still a long way off, his father saw him and felt compassion for him, and ran and embraced him and kissed him. And the son said to him, "Father, I have sinned against heaven and in your sight; I am no longer worthy to be called your son." But the father said to his slaves, "Quickly bring out the best robe and put it on him, and put a ring on his finger and sandals on his feet; and bring the fattened calf, slaughter it, and let's eat and celebrate; for this son of mine was dead and has come to life again; he was lost and has been found." And they began to celebrate. (Luke 15:20–24)

The son headed home, and as soon as the father saw him coming over the hill, he did something that would have been socially unacceptable. A respectable, honorable father, especially one with such wealth, would have sat back and waited for the son to arrive. It would be up to the son to come in a respectful manner all the way to the father. Then the father would determine whether he would receive him or not.

It was unimaginable that a man of his stature would take off running toward the son. But the father wasn't interested in what was socially correct. His heart was filled with love and compassion for his son. He ran and embraced him. At this point, the father didn't know the son's intentions. For all he knew, the son was coming back to ask for more money. But he loved his son, and his son had returned home—and at that moment, that was all that mattered.

The son began to deliver his rehearsed speech. But only a few words in, the father had heard enough to know his son was repentant, and that was what he needed to hear. He ordered the finest robe to be brought for his son. He put a ring on his finger and sandals on his feet. He killed the fattened calf and threw a party. Why? Because his son had been lost but now had come home.

His older son, meanwhile, remained outside, disapproving.

Grace Is Confusing

The parable of the prodigal son is familiar to most Christians. We like the story, but it's important to understand that the first-century religious crowd would have been appalled by the father's response. It wasn't right. The son had broken the Law (working for a Gentile, handling religiously unclean animals, etc.), and a good Jewish father would have administered strict punishment.

(Now, just to be clear, the son in the parable was an adult, so the dynamics in the story would not be those of a father failing to discipline his young son, as we discussed in the previous chapter. This story is not intended to be a parable about parenting young children. Jesus is illustrating why He was eating with sinners and tax collectors. Justice makes sense. Grace is confusing.)

We shouldn't be too quick to judge the religious leaders of Jesus' day. I'm pretty sure that if we told a twenty-first-century version of the story, we might struggle with the father's reaction too. He's enabling his son, we'd say. Choices must have consequences for the boy to learn. He's rewarding reckless behavior.

To be honest, the father's reaction doesn't feel right. As a matter of fact, if you attended church with this father, it's possible that you, too, might have chosen to remain outside the party with the older brother, for some very spiritual-sounding reasons. Me too. Whether it's a father with his young children or an adult son like in the parable, grace is puzzling.

Grace doesn't line up with how we view the world. In this story, Jesus was explaining why He spent time with sinners, misfits, and losers. People like us. The answer, in a word: grace.

If we have experienced God's salvation and have right standing before Him, it's only on the basis of His grace. We deserve condemnation. Despite this, He offers reconciliation. God doesn't sit back and make us grovel and crawl back. He runs to meet us and welcome us home with open arms. We deserve darkness, but He invites us into the light. What a beautiful and compelling picture of God.

Talking versus Living

Here's the big question: Is that your view of God? I mean, really. Do you see God as gracious and forgiving, longing to spend time with you simply because He treasures you? Do you see God running to meet you after you've blown it (again)?

Many Christians in their most honest moments would admit that this is not their view of God. Why is that? There's a pretty good chance that it's because this is not the picture that was painted for you at home. That's our focus in this chapter.

Over the years, I've concluded that many Christians don't really believe what they say they believe. We know the words and we talk the talk, but we don't really believe it. Perhaps nowhere is this more evident than in our theology of grace.

Philip Yancey quotes a well-known pastor and counselor who summed up his career this way:

> Many years ago I was driven to the conclusion that the two major causes of most emotional problems among evangelical Christians are these: the failure to understand, receive and live out God's unconditional grace and forgiveness, and the failure to give out that unconditional love, forgiveness and grace to other people.... We read, we hear, we believe a good theology of grace. But that's not the way we live.[1]

Many struggle along with a messed-up view of God because they grew up in an environment of "ungrace." Such kids grow up and either pass their rigidity and legalism on to the next generation or walk away from God and church because it feels too much like the oppression they grew up under. Either way, their view of God is warped and destructive.

There is no detour around grace to get to a meaningful Christian life. A right understanding of grace is the key that unlocks the life for which our souls long. If you don't truly believe in a God who is amazingly gracious, you'll never feel comfortable in His presence.

I have devoted the rest of this chapter to making sure we understand grace: what it is and what it isn't, and how it gets pictured at home. If your picture of God doesn't match that of the father in the Prodigal Son story, you have work to do. So let's get to it.

For Freedom

Grace has been the subject of entire books. It's a big topic. In *God's Not Like That*, we will limit our study to ways grace is (or isn't) experienced at home. After four decades of trying to help people experience the joy they desire in Christ, I have learned that the issues related to grace and the operating system at home top the list for impacting our view of God.

Paul states, "It was for freedom that Christ set us free; therefore keep standing firm and do not be subject again to a yoke of slavery" (Gal. 5:1). Interestingly, we are *commanded* to keep standing firm. In other words, if we were to go back to a yoke of slavery, it would be an act of disobedience.

If you don't truly believe in a God who is amazingly gracious, you'll never feel comfortable in His presence.

It's been my experience that many Christians don't so much go back to slavery as they fail to embrace the freedom granted in Christ. It's more like the cage door has been opened but we choose to remain locked up. Why is that? Often, it's because of subtle lessons we learned about God growing up.

Correction or Punishment?

Let's start with how discipline was administered at home. This ties in with the previous chapter, where we focused on fathers and discipline. Here, I want to zoom in on discipline and specifically how it impacts our view of the God of grace. Parents are to represent the way God disciplines His children. So here's our starting question: Is the primary purpose of discipline to correct or to punish? The difference matters.

According to the Bible, our salvation is provided by God's amazing grace. It's not Jesus plus our religion that obtains salvation, or Jesus plus our good works ... or Jesus plus anything. "For by grace you have been saved through faith; and this is not of yourselves, it is the gift of God; not a result of works, so that no one may boast" (Eph. 2:8–9).

Paul states that we have been "justified by faith" (Rom. 5:1). *Justified* is a legal term that means "declared right before a holy God."[2] How? Not by our works but by faith in Jesus and His work on the cross.

> And when you were dead in your wrongdoings ...
> He made you alive together with Him, having for-
> given us all our wrongdoings, having canceled the

certificate of debt consisting of decrees against us,
which was hostile to us; and He has taken it out of
the way, having nailed it to the cross. (Col. 2:13–14)

The result is that "there is now no condemnation at all for those who are in Christ Jesus" (Rom. 8:1). In other words, on the cross, Jesus took my punishment upon Himself. He paid the price for my sin. I became justified, made right before God, and therefore I am no longer condemned. This is equally true on my best days and my worst days.

So when I sin or go astray, God doesn't punish me for my sin. Jesus already took that punishment for me. But God may indeed bring discipline to me. He may correct me for my own good. It's corrective, not punitive. The difference is important.

When the Prodigal Son returned to his father, there was deep repentance in his attitude. He had blown his inheritance and made a mess of his life. The heart of the father was not to make his son pay for his sin but to cause him to learn from his sin. His desire was to correct the path his son was on so he would experience life rather than misery. This is why he welcomed his son back rather than punishing him. This is how Jesus receives us as repentant sinners.

The responsibility of the parent is to portray this grace at home. Discipline should be about teaching and correcting. As a dad, I'm far more interested in correcting bad behavior than simply punishing it. I'm not trying to make my child pay for crimes as with a jail sentence. The correction I bring is not punitive. It's not condemnation. It's teaching and correcting.

The truth is that even as a child of God, I may still blow it today. I may sin and offend God, hurting myself and those around me. Yet, in that moment, *I still stand righteous* before a holy God. Why? Because of my works? No, my works were terrible today. But because Jesus died to pay for my sin, and today there is no condemnation to those in Christ Jesus. Amazing! All Jesus.

How does this impact parenting? Let me see if I can illustrate. Years ago, when one of my girls was in high school, she had driven into town for an activity. We live about twenty miles out of town. She was a very responsible teenager. But on this particular week-night, when it was time for her to be home, she wasn't back yet.

You can picture the conversation that happened at our home. Patti was getting concerned. I was saying, "You know, honey, let's just take a deep breath and give it a little time here." But it got later and later. We called our daughter's cell phone but got no answer. We were always concerned about the drive through the country after dark. She could get in an accident, have car trouble, or hit a deer. She wasn't normally late, and she always had her cell phone on, so this was odd.

It finally got late enough that we determined something had to be wrong, so we got in the car and headed for town. Of course, our minds were already going to the worst-case scenario. We were expecting to go up over a hill and see red flashing lights because there had been an accident or there was a car upside down in a ditch somewhere. The tension built with every passing mile. We got probably about two-thirds of the way into town when we passed her coming home, so we turned around.

In that moment, there was a great sense of relief, but the fear that had been churning turned into other emotions that weren't going to be productive. When we pulled into the driveway, I said to Patti, "Honey, you're pretty stressed right now. Would you just let me talk to her?" She agreed.

We got into the house and sat down, and I said to my daughter, "Where were you?" She said she was at youth group and afterwards she had a couple of friends who were going through some hard things and wanted to talk about it. She didn't realize her phone was off. She had lost track of time and suddenly realized it was late and came home.

In that moment, all I needed was to see in her eyes a recognition that her lack of communication was unacceptable. What she did for her friends was commendable, but she would need to communicate better, especially when driving twenty miles home alone after dark. I explained to her that she was growing up and would have more freedom, but with that came responsibility. I told her she'd have to do better if we were going to trust her. The look in her eyes said, "Dad, I understand, and it won't happen again."

The whole conversation took less than fifteen minutes. I gave her a hug and told her I loved her, and we went to bed, confident that she understood.

Two or three days later, my daughter said, "Dad, my friends are blown away that I am not grounded."

"What do you mean?" I asked.

"My friends said they would have been grounded for a week if they had done something like that."

I smiled. "Honey, the thing that mattered that night was that you understood that what happened was not acceptable. It can't happen again. When I saw that you heard me and understood, that was all I needed. End of story."

Was that just? Did the punishment fit the crime? Probably not. But it never happened again. It was correction, not punishment. My intent was to teach, not to make her pay. Isn't that how God parents us? Isn't that grace?

When we *don't* understand grace, we spend too much time in the dark. We wallow in our shame and guilt. We beat ourselves up for sins Jesus already paid for. We hide in a dark room because we think we need to punish ourselves for our failures. We're trying to earn some measure of forgiveness. We feel we need to convince God of how sorry we are. We believe we deserve a time-out in the darkness. We may interpret everything bad in our lives as God making us pay for past sins. This creates a fearful and oppressive view of God.

Honestly, how much time do you spend in the dark room nursing your shame and guilt? How readily do you beat yourself up for past mistakes? Do you struggle to accept the forgiveness and grace of Jesus? Do you interpret every bad thing in your life as God punishing you for past sins? Why is that? Where did you learn that?

Earlier, we learned we were created to dance with God. This is where we find the life for which our soul longs. Imagine I get to the end of a lousy day where I've blown it and made a mess of things. I put myself in the dark room because of my shame and guilt. I think I need to be punished.

But then I remember the amazing grace of God and that my sin has been paid for, so I run out of the dark room, down the hall, and into the light room. There, I see Jesus like the father of the Prodigal Son waiting for me. I jump into His waiting arms, and we dance together to the music of "Amazing Grace."

I can imagine some people appalled by that imagery. What about confession and repentance? Agreed. But true confession and repentance don't happen in the dark room. The dark room is filled with excuses, rationalizations, and hiding. Nothing good happens in that darkness. We go there to punish ourselves because we messed up again. But my sin has already been paid for. We need correction, not condemnation. True confession and repentance happen as the light of Jesus shines on our sin (John 3:19–21). Grace is permission to run to the light, even on our worst days. This is what makes grace so life changing.

What was the environment like at home for you? Was discipline focused on teaching and correction or punishing? Today, do you feel like God is always lurking in the shadows waiting to punish you for your latest blunder? I talked with a young father some time back who believed his baby died because God was punishing him for past sins. Is that really how God operates? God's not like that. Why did he believe that? Most of the time, those beliefs root back to our family of origin.

Internal or External

Correction or punishment ties in with the next area of focus. Does real life change come from external pressures or internal transformation? Grace is at the foundation of what we believe as Christians.

This is not a do-it-yourself religion. Our simple message is that we are sinners in need of a Savior. No matter who you are, what you've done, or how good you may think you are, your only hope is Jesus.

The Bible is clear: works cannot make us right before God. No amount of religious behavior, rule-keeping, or good intentions will save us. God does not grade on a curve. We are saved only by grace through faith.

External pressures or systems cannot change the human heart. The Jewish Law could not and cannot make anyone acceptable before a holy God, nor can any law of the land. This is key for our discussion. Real change comes from the inside out through Jesus, not through well-intended efforts or religious works. This is not a performance-based religion.[3]

Paul could not be clearer on this:

> A person is not justified by works of the Law but through faith in Christ Jesus, even we have believed in Christ Jesus, so that we may be justified by faith in Christ and not by works of the Law; since by works of the Law no flesh will be justified. (Gal. 2:16)

"Religion" tries to modify the exterior. It's a man-made remodeling of sorts, but it offers no internal transformation. New birth is what we need: a change from the inside out that can come only by grace through faith.

The Bible teaches that true heart change does not happen through law-keeping (external) but by the power of the Spirit in us. Paul told the Galatians that it's foolish to think that what God started by the Spirit can be completed by the flesh. Yet for some reason, at home, we often revert to a law-based system.

So here's a question to ponder: How well does the biblical truth concerning heart change align with how we parent? In other words, is the environment at home more focused on compliance to the rules (law-keeping) or cultivating the spiritual life within?

There are certainly things about an external compliance approach that are appealing. It tends to be pretty black and white: we lay down the rules, and if you break them, here are the consequences. This approach rates high on clarity and doesn't require much investment of time or relationship. This approach is convenient for busy families.

The downside, however, is worth underscoring. If the goal is heart change, this method doesn't work. You can get compliance with this system, but not lasting change. This is part of our core theology as Christians: law-keeping doesn't change the heart.

It should be noted that there are challenges with the *internal* approach too. It's more subjective. It can get messy and uncertain at times. It's a long-term strategy that takes a lot of patience, thoughtfulness, and relationship. And it's not going to work well in the fast lane. It's discipleship, and that takes time.

But the impact is internal heart change, which leads to life.

A grace-based environment at home flows out of the deep conviction that true life change comes from the internal work of the Spirit and not through law-keeping. This will impact every decision made at home.

Compliance versus Direction

Years ago, I was introduced to a couple of diagrams from the world
of sociology that help illustrate the difference between these two
approaches. One is an illustration of what's called a bounded set,
and the other depicts a center set.

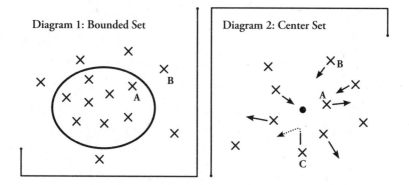

The *bounded set* (diagram 1) is defined by a boundary made up of
rules and expectations. You are either in or out based on your performance. The focus is on compliance. If you are inside the boundary,
everything is fine. If you are outside the boundary, external pressures are required to force you into compliance. Often, shame is the
weapon of choice for this.

Many churches and families function this way. We would
view these environments as legalistic, and as such there are many
problems with this approach. Perhaps the most significant problem, as we've already seen, is that compliance isn't heart change. It
may bring the parents a false sense of security from thinking that
everything is fine simply because someone is coloring within the

lines. Sometimes, these kids leave home and go wild, leaving the parents to wonder what happened. Too often, forcing children into compliance in childhood causes them to become rebellious as they grow older.

The alternative is called a *center set* (diagram 2). In this approach, the key is to define the center or the goal. This is the bull's-eye of the target. Perhaps for our purposes, we would say the center is the goal to be like Jesus.

In this model, the focus is on momentum. In which direction is the person going? Are they trending toward the middle or away from it? This is not to imply that there are no rules or guidelines—it simply illustrates where the emphasis lies. The conversation is not about *in* or *out* but direction and movement. Strategically, the mission is to get the momentum headed in the right direction.

These diagrams are helpful for understanding our strategy both at home and in the church. A focus on the externals will cause us to concentrate on making sure there is compliance to the rules. Stay in the boundary. If someone strays beyond the fence, we'll do what is necessary to bring them back into compliance. A focus on the heart is more concerned with which direction the person is moving in. We know that as long as someone is headed toward the center, necessary changes will come about over time. As long as the momentum is in the right direction, we have reason to be encouraged.

The difference between these two approaches is significant. Let me illustrate. Many preachers use a model like this: "For this sermon, do my listeners most need to understand this truth, believe this truth, or apply this truth?" I think of this as three levels:

Level one: understand

Level two: believe

Level three: apply

Every week as a teacher of God's Word, I wrestle with this question. If what is needed most is understanding, I'll spend most of my time explaining. If what's needed is belief, I'll seek to convince. If it's application, I'll illustrate and give practical steps. But even when I choose one of the three emphases over the other two, I'm aware—and this is key—that all three are necessary. People won't live out what they don't believe, and they'll struggle to believe what they don't understand.

To apply this grid to our two diagrams, we could say that the bounded set focuses primarily on level three: application (behavior). It's all about what you do and don't do. Here are the rules and expectations. Do as we tell you. Stay within the boundary—that's what matters. The truth that drives or motivates the behavior may not be clear or even necessary. You just do as you're told.

How many Christians live within the boundaries and follow the rules without really understanding why? Many could not open their Bibles and explain the truth behind why they live the way they live. For many, the answer would simply be because that's what they were told and pressured to conform to.

The center set, on the other hand, is primarily focused on levels one and two, understanding and belief. "Here's what is true of you in Christ. If you truly believe it, you'll live like it." Obedience is the outflow of understanding and believing the truth. This is true heart change that motivates a life of obedience from the inside out. One is law-keeping, the other is grace.

Look back at the bounded set diagram. Imagine two children: A and B. One (A) appears acceptable because they are inside the boundary, but the other (B), not so much. Yet in reality, that may not be the case. Perhaps child A is simply more compliant by nature. Perhaps child A has learned to play the game better than child B. Maybe the real difference between them is negligible. Remember, compliance to the rules signifies no more than that: compliance to the rules. It doesn't mean anything of significance is happening in cultivating a heart to follow Jesus.

Now notice children A and B in the diagram of the center set. One is far off but headed toward the center, and one is closer but headed away. Which one should be the greater concern? Think how different this looks from the bounded set, which may give us a false reading of who's doing well and who is not. There may be many things about child B that still need to change, but as long as their momentum continues toward the center, those things will be resolved over time. We call this *discipleship*. It's not necessary to fix everything right now. Strategically, just get the momentum going in the right direction and cheerlead the progress.

People won't live out what they don't believe, and they'll struggle to believe what they don't understand.

Now look at child C in the center set diagram. Notice the change of direction. He was headed the right way and had good momentum, but something—perhaps too much pressure to conform to the boundary—triggered the change. That's a strategic error, and now you have a much bigger problem. Try to change too much too fast, and rebellion is likely to occur. Sadly, it wasn't necessary. The momentum was carrying them in the right direction. A little patience could have made a big difference.

Why did this happen? Often, it's because the parent is more concerned with conforming to the prescribed standard (the boundary) than cultivating the heart. The focus is more on application than understanding. In other words, looking good is more important than being good. External over internal.

When the external matters more at home than the internal, how we look is very important. Paul refers to legalism as a desire "to make a good showing in the flesh" (Gal. 6:12). Jesus accused the Pharisees of doing their deeds to be noticed by others (Matt. 23:5; Luke 11:43). That's external over internal. How many families make a grand appearance at church, looking very spiritual, but are a dysfunctional mess at home?

Think about the story of the Prodigal Son. What the father celebrated was movement in the right direction. The inheritance was gone, and the son really had made a mess of things. But he was coming home, and that was what the father desired most. Remember, Jesus told that parable to explain to the religious leaders why He spent so much time with sinners and tax collectors. What was He really saying?

On another occasion, Jesus was more to the point:

> Woe to you, scribes and Pharisees, hypocrites!
> For you are like whitewashed tombs which on the
> outside appear beautiful, but inside they are full
> of dead men's bones and all uncleanness. So you
> too, outwardly appear righteous to people, but
> inwardly you are full of hypocrisy and lawless-
> ness. (Matt. 23:27–28)

Think about where the Pharisees would land in the bounded set (diagram 1). They would appear to be righteous because they were inside the boundary. Yet, according to Jesus, they were far from God. Where would the sinners and tax collectors appear on the diagram? This illustrates how the Jewish people would have viewed both the religious leaders and the sinners and tax collectors. Yet, obviously, Jesus saw the situation quite differently.

Now place the Pharisees and sinners in the center set (diagram 2). What is the direction of momentum for each group? Which diagram more accurately reflects the truth of what was happening? Which of these two groups loved and pursued Jesus more?

Why did the religious leaders experience so much anger and conflict with Jesus, while sinners, misfits, and losers couldn't get enough of Him? What was it about Jesus that made Him so attractive to hurting, messed-up people? In a word, grace.

Is that how Jesus was pictured to you at home? Which diagram better mirrors life in your family of origin, and how might that have influenced your view of God? Is your Christian life defined more by rule-keeping or a love relationship? As a Christian, are you more motivated to look good in certain environments or to be genuinely good from the inside out?

Performance or Relationship

The last theme we want to examine has to do with the basis of our significance and value. Was your significance growing up determined by your performance or relationship—by what you did or by whose you are?

Before the fall, people made in the image of God were created to find their significance and value in being rightly related to God. After our separation from God, the temptation became to function as our own god and make ourselves valuable and significant. This is done through our ability to perform and assessing how we compete and compare to those around us. This is the world's operating system. It's a journey to find significance and value apart from a relationship with God.

You might be surprised to learn how subtly we reinforce the world's operating system at home. This is often done by loving and caring parents who desire to celebrate and encourage their children. They are good people wanting to do the right thing. But the world's operating system is so familiar that we don't always know we're using it. It seems normal.

Of course, there are other parents who are desperately trying to be somebody through their children and their achievements, and still others who operate out of their own deep hurts, insecurities, and unhappiness with life. In all these scenarios, we can be sure that the default mode at home is a performance-based value system. To be fair, nobody naturally leans toward a grace-based system. It has to be curated with great intentionality.

In most cases, a performance-based value system is introduced and reinforced early on at home. Consider this: Little Susie wins the third-grade spelling bee. Are we excited that Susie won the spelling bee? Yes, we should be. Good for her. So, at supper that night, there's a big party. Little Susie won the spelling bee! Yay! Congratulations. Susie picks up on the fact that Mom and Dad seem a little more excited about *her* as a result of her victory.

A couple of days later, the parents have some friends over, and Susie hears her mom say more than once, "Oh, by the way, did you hear that our Susie is the spelling bee champion?" Susie knows that it's been awhile since her mom bragged on her like that, and it feels good. Mom and Dad seem to be really excited about Susie now. A couple of weeks later, they go to visit Grandma and Grandpa, and the first thing Grandma says is, "There's my little spelling bee champion!"

Do you hear what's happening? Everyone is excited and wants to be affirming. That's wonderful. But what is Susie hearing? Clearly, the message she can't miss is that when she performs well, the people around her are more excited about her. In her mind, could that be telling her that when she excels, they value her—or even love her—more? Might she start to think that as long as she keeps performing well, her mom and dad will value her more? That's the subtle message.

Now to be clear, the issue is not performance. We should seek to be the best version of ourselves we can be. I'm also not suggesting we shouldn't celebrate and encourage our kids' accomplishments. The issue I'm talking about is using performance as the basis of our value and significance apart from God. Of course we want to encourage and celebrate our kids. We should. But we need to work to be sure our subtle messaging is not, "I am what I do." That's the risk.

I can hear someone saying, "Oh, that's a silly concern." But is it? Every environment Susie experiences will reinforce that subtle message. School, sports, music, dance, report card, cheerleader, job, homecoming queen, and on it goes. You tell me: What's a child to conclude? This is the dominant messaging in our culture: your significance and value come from how you perform, how you compete and compare with others. This value system will be reinforced countless times before a child leaves home.

And what about when she fails to do well? What about the siblings who can't compete at that level? What about the average kid who isn't super-smart or talented? What about the struggler at home? How many kids have tried and failed to be like their gifted brothers or sisters who seem to be getting all the attention? So many of us learned early in life that we don't measure up according to the world's performance-based value system.

And what about the parent who's never satisfied with his or her child's performance? The parent for whom good enough will never be good enough? Push, push, push. How about the dad who wanted a linebacker but got a show choir son? What about the mom who needs the kids to be the best in everything or needs her girls to be homecoming queen or in the popular crowd? What about the parents who are determined that their children get straight A's and graduate at the top of the class to prove something? The pressure to perform is all too real.

How could this approach *not* encourage a performance-based value system? The message at home seems to align with the voices of the culture, making a very compelling case that my value and significance comes from what I do rather than my identity in Christ.

Consider little Johnnie. He's struggling with his self-esteem, and his mom and dad are concerned. They love Johnnie, but he simply isn't as talented as his older sister. So, in order to build Johnnie's self-esteem, they point to something Johnnie is good at. "You know, you're really good at coloring. Color some pictures, and we'll put them on the refrigerator."

What we are saying to Johnnie is that he does have significance and value because there is something he can do really well. We're planting a seed in his mind that value comes from what you do. That message gets reinforced over and over, and Johnnie gets it. He figures out that if he's good at something, he has value. That makes sense because it lines up with all the voices of the culture. Johnnie has bought into a value system that will eventually leave him empty and disappointed when he finds out there are plenty of others who color better than he does.

A performance-based value system is at the core of so many of our struggles in life. It may determine the house we buy or the car we drive. What about the career we choose or how we spend our money? We feel the pressure to compete and compare all day long, and it's exhausting. We suffer from various forms of performance anxiety and low self-esteem. We try and try and try, but it's never enough. We long for approval but it feels like the elusive carrot on a string. We're weary, but there's no rest. No peace.

Of course, when the operating system at home is performance-based, all these wrong ideas get projected onto God. We fall into legalistic patterns, thinking that the only way to please God is to perform. God is like that parent who is never satisfied. Good enough will never be good enough. It feels like God is always disappointed with us. We're desperately trying to find that thing we can do well enough to make God proud. We serve Him to gain His approval. We want Him to hang the pictures we colored on the refrigerator, but there's always someone else's pictures that are better than ours.

Do you feel that? Do you struggle to measure up? Do you experience anxiety because you're not good enough, pretty enough, smart enough, successful enough, or spiritual enough? This drains the life out of your Christian walk and steals your joy. This makes God seem oppressive rather than loving. We're so busy trying to earn God's favor that we fail to simply delight in His presence by grace through faith.

Why do we struggle so? Where did we learn this value system? Why do we think we have to perform in order for God to be pleased with us? Why does the basis of our significance and value seem more like a page out of the playbook of the world than something made possible by amazing grace? I believe it goes back to our family of origin.

The alternative, of course, is a culture of grace. Of intentionally focusing on relationship over performance. It's about finding our identity in Christ as a child of God. As discussed above, it's about seeking to create an environment at home that recognizes the importance of the inner life of the Spirit. It's valuing the person over performance. It's being more about who you are than what you do. Internal over external. This lays the foundation from which the other voices can be interpreted.

Christian parents need to fly in a direction that is contrary to the culture. They need to point to God as the basis of their children's significance and value. They need to model this in their own lives. They need to seize teachable moments to explain and illustrate what grace looks like in real-life situations.

This implies that parents understand and live according to grace themselves. You can't teach what you don't understand. This is often where the breakdown occurs.

As we've said before, our parents were themselves parented by someone. The world's performance-based operating system is so common that most pass it along without even knowing it's there. It seems normal. These parents can be good people trying hard to do what is best for their kids, without ever gaining the awareness that a performance-based system sets kids up for disappointment as adults.

But even for parents who have a strong understanding of grace, creating a grace-based value system at home is not easy. As a matter of fact, it is extremely difficult. You are swimming upstream, and the current is very strong. Every other environment you enter is likely to reinforce the world's performance-based value system. It starts to feel like it's you against the world—and in some ways, it is.

However, it's good to remember two things. First, God is on your side. You have the supernatural presence of the Holy Spirit, and that makes all the difference. Second, a parent's voice can be the strongest, most compelling voice to children, especially when the kids are young. A parent's voice is not just another voice in a sea of noise. A parent is uniquely positioned to influence a child's view of God.

Whether it's little Susie and her spelling bee or little Johnnie as an average performer, a grace-based value system at home lays the foundation for processing all other environments. Achievements can be enjoyed and celebrated without becoming the basis of one's significance. Being average or below average doesn't have to mean we are any less significant or have less value. It just means we're average or below average when it comes to that particular comparison. Our self-esteem doesn't have to go up and down every day but can remain grounded in who we are in Christ on the basis of God's grace.

How many Christians will spend a lifetime trying to prove they have value ... to people who don't really care? How many will agonize to gain favor from a God who already loves them, accepts them, and celebrates them in Christ? How many Christians can truly rest in the amazing grace of God on both their best days and their worst days? Whichever pattern defines your life, it's highly likely that the roots of your thinking reach back into your family of origin and reflect your view of God.

God's Masterpiece

Let me close this chapter with a picture of how God views you as His child. To be clear, if you are a child of God, this *is* how God views you. How does this truth line up with what you experienced in your family of origin and how you believe God views you today?

The first two chapters of Ephesians are absolutely magnificent. They are two of my favorite chapters in all of the Bible. Ephesians 1:6 tells us that we were saved "to the praise of the glory of [God's] grace." Have you ever wrestled with the question "Why would God lavish His riches upon me?" The answer is, to put His grace on display and give Himself glory.

Here's the news flash: It isn't really about you. It's about God and His grace put on display in order that He might receive praise. Remarkably, we are simply the recipients of a treasure that seems incomprehensible.

Ephesians 2 tells us that we were dead in sin and by nature children of wrath:

> You were dead in your offenses and sins, in which you previously walked according to the course of this world, according to the prince of the power of the air, of the spirit that is now working in the sons of disobedience. Among them we too all previously lived in the lusts of our flesh, indulging the desires of the flesh and of the mind, and were by nature children of wrath, just as the rest. (vv. 1–3)

Paul uses the imagery of us being dead to remind us that we were incapable of rescuing ourselves. You couldn't have done it—you were dead. I was as hopeless as hopeless could possibly be. Then Paul gets to this incredible theology:

> But God, being rich in mercy, because of His great love with which He loved us, even when we were dead in our wrongdoings, made us alive together with Christ (by grace you have been saved), and raised us up with Him, and seated us with Him in the heavenly places in Christ Jesus, so that in the ages to come He might show the boundless riches of His grace in kindness toward us in Christ Jesus. For by grace you have been saved through faith; and this is not of yourselves, it is the gift of God; not a result of works, so that no one may boast. (vv. 4–9)

You can't miss that the emphasis is grace, grace, grace, grace, grace. God did it all. You did nothing. You can't boast about it. All God! That's the whole point of the text: You were dead. God did it all. It was amazing grace that saved a wretch like me.

Then Paul gives us this awesome crescendo: "For we are His workmanship, created in Christ Jesus for good works, which God prepared beforehand so that we would walk in them" (v. 10).

You, on the basis of God's grace, are God's original creation! Behind the English word *workmanship* is the Greek word *poema*. It means "something created by craftsmen, like an original piece of art or music or poetry."[4] New Testament scholar F. F. Bruce translates it, "His work of art, His masterpiece."[5] God has made you His masterpiece of grace, so magnificent that when He holds you up in the heavenlies, the angels will gasp at the wonder of what you've become (Eph. 2:6–7; Col. 3:4). Why would God do this? So He could put His grace on display in order to bring Himself glory. Through no effort or merit of your own, you stand utterly magnificent before God.

God's Inheritance

This is the truth: you are God's masterpiece. God delights in you. He sings over you (Zeph. 3:17). It's not that God tolerates you or puts up with you. He *celebrates* you. As a matter of fact, Paul talks about you as "the glory of His inheritance in the saints" (Eph. 1:11–14, 18). It's not that you *get* an inheritance (though that is true)—what Ephesians is saying is that you *are* the inheritance![6]

Think of everything in the universe in which God could and does delight. For example, consider this the next time you are sitting on top of a mountain overwhelmed by the beauty of what God has created. Or the next time you are consumed by the beauty of a sunset or the majesty of the ocean. Remember, of everything God created, the thing He most treasures is you![7] You are His inheritance. You are His favorite! You are His masterpiece! Not the mountains. Not the ocean. Not the solar system. Of everything God has made, you are His work of art, and He delights in you!

> God has made you His masterpiece of grace, so magnificent that when He holds you up in the heavenlies, the angels will gasp at the wonder of what you've become.

God celebrates you unlike anyone else celebrates you. It is the most wondrous, unimaginable, scandalous truth ever. We take by faith that God tells the truth. He means what He says. That's how He sees you, and it's not based on your performance. It's amazing grace.

Every time I go through that passage, it breathes life into my spirit. Nobody sees me as God sees me. There's nobody in this world who celebrates me as God does. At the end of the story, there will be only one opinion that matters. That one opinion is God's, and it is He who sees me most magnificently. That brings tears to my eyes. It impacts me deeply because nobody else will ever see me that way.

Grace at Home

Do you really believe that's how God views you? Do you see God that way? True grace at home is rare. However, rightly pictured, it is life-changing for everyone involved. Grace, understood and lived out, could be the key that unlocks the life your soul longs for. It frees you to perform at your best for all the right reasons. Because your significance and value are no longer at risk, you are at peace in the presence of God.

We've covered a lot in this chapter. A weak theology of grace leads to a frustrating and disappointing Christian life. The world's operating system will let you down in the end. It has no winners. Because we've covered so much here, you may need to take some extra time to consider what you experienced in your family of origin and how it lines up with the truth of God's amazing grace. *It was for freedom that Christ set us free.*

Reflecting on
My Family of Origin

Before reading this book, what was your belief regarding how God views you? Does God delight in you, or do you feel He is angry with you or embarrassed and frustrated by you?

Did you grow up in an environment more like the bounded set or the center set? What message did that communicate to you about your acceptance before God?

Was there more emphasis in your home on looking good or on being good? Was there more emphasis on growing your relationship with Jesus or on following the rules?

Was discipline at home more about teaching or punishment? Corrective or punitive?

Were you valued at home for your performance or your relationship? Did you feel pressure to measure up? What was celebrated, posted, or applauded in your home growing up?

Today, do you spend more time in the dark room or the light room? Why is that?

Think about words that honestly describe your view of God before you read this chapter on grace.

What would be alternative words to correct a misperception of God?

One of our goals in cultivating an accurate view of God is that our hearts would reflect the compassion and grace of Jesus. How does this chapter inform our response to our parents and what we experienced growing up? What practical steps can you take to represent the grace of Jesus to those who raised you?

Journal Entry

Write a paragraph describing how you believed God views you before reading this chapter.

Now, based on this chapter, write a more accurate description of how God views you through the lens of amazing grace.

Which paragraph will you choose to believe?

Chapter 9

Afterwards

Prayer comes hard for me. Maybe that seems like an odd thing for a pastor to admit, but it's true. I had been a pastor for many years before I realized how my life growing up had impacted my struggle with prayer.

For over twenty years, I watched my dad struggle. He was confined to a bed and in intense pain every moment of every day. As a child, I prayed every night. I begged God to do something to make it stop. It didn't stop. I knew lots of godly men and women who prayed faithfully for healing, but the healing never came, at least not in this life.

It never crossed my mind how much that experience impacted my motivation to pray as an adult. I loved Jesus and was bent on serving Him. I had worked through my struggles trying to reconcile the idea of a loving God with what I had witnessed growing up. But I had never connected the dots between my childhood and my prayer life.

One day, I was preparing to preach a sermon series on prayer when I realized I was struggling to believe some of what I was about to teach. *What's the point of praying if it doesn't change anything?* I caught myself thinking. *How many times can a child be disappointed before it hurts too much to hope again?* I realized that at some point, I had given up. What was the use of prayer? I mean, how could prayer actually move the hand of a sovereign God? It can't, or so I had concluded.

The problem with that view is that it simply doesn't line up with what God says in His Word (Ex. 32:14; Matt. 7:7–8; Phil. 4:6; James 4:2). There were those nagging scriptures that say that prayer sometimes *does* move the hand of God. My experiences at home as a child had taught me something about God that isn't true. My conclusions were either (1) that God doesn't hear, (2) that He doesn't care, or (3) that He lacks the power to do anything. Bottom line, I had determined that prayer doesn't work. It's hard to get motivated to do something you believe doesn't work.

Once I realized how my experiences growing up had impacted my view of God and prayer, I was able to correct my errors and embrace the truth. I do believe God hears our prayers. I do believe He cares. And I do believe that He certainly has the power to respond to any situation. His answer may be no or not yet, but I do believe my prayers can move the hand of a sovereign God. How it all works, I don't know. But today I choose to believe it.

What Do We Believe?

So, what do you believe? We Christians get pretty good at saying the right things. We sing about how much we trust God and how willing we are to surrender all to God. We say we will praise Him in the storm and bless His holy name no matter what. We may be very sincere when we say these words. But do we really believe?

It's not that we are trying to be rebellious. We don't want to disbelieve. Rather, so often we simply aren't aware of what we do and don't believe about God. The messaging can be so subtle based on experiences growing up. My parents weren't to blame for my confusion about prayer. They couldn't help the way things were. It was simply my conclusion based on the circumstances.

As I've said before, your family did not have to be abusive or dysfunctional to teach you things about God that aren't true. You may have come from a warm, loving, caring family. You love your parents dearly, and they did so many good things for you growing up. It's wonderful if you had a family like that. But there can still be things you learned about God at home that have misshaped your view of Him.

For example, think about how trials and hardships were handled at home. Was God trusted … or blamed? Was there peace or fear? Did it feel like your house was built on rock or sand? There's a lot of theology that is passed on to kids at the family dinner table. What was that experience like for you?

Perhaps, like me, your prayers went unanswered, which caused you to formulate a view of God that isn't accurate. Maybe there was abuse in the home and you begged God to make it stop, but it didn't stop. Maybe you asked God to heal your parents' marriage, but they divorced instead. What if you prayed every night for God to give you a happy family but you got an angry family? What if a parent or sibling died of a painful disease or your beloved pet was run over by a car? Think about it. How does all this impact our view of God?

What Do I Believe about God?

It's not easy to determine what you really believe about God. How do you know if you hold beliefs about Him that aren't accurate?

One thing I've found helpful is to wrestle with this question: "What would cause me to hesitate to surrender fully to God?" The only reason I can think of is if I don't trust Him. In some part of my mind, I must be believing something about God that isn't true, something that is causing me to doubt. There's nothing in the character of God that should cause me to hesitate to trust Him. So, if I'm not willing to surrender fully to God, there must be some belief I hold about God that is not correct.

Maybe I don't trust God to meet my needs or my desires for happiness, pleasure, or significance. Therefore, I'm tempted to take charge of those areas of my life and do it my way. But why can't God be trusted in those areas? Why do I think He'll let me down? Why does it feel so hard to trust Him? Your feelings can help unearth your beliefs.

I know I want to be my own god, but why? Logically, I know I can't offer myself more than what God offers me—not even close. I know I'm tragically inadequate compared to God, yet I insist on doing things my own way. Why? Am I simply defective or stubbornly bent on rebellion, or is it possible that, deep down, I believe things about God that aren't true, and that this is what prevents me from surrendering to Him? In reality, there is nothing in the character of God that should cause us to hesitate to trust Him.

So why do we hold back? Why do we seem so determined to run our own lives? We all naturally bend in that direction, apart from

Christ. As people made in the image of God, we have the ability and responsibility to represent God to the world. The temptation that can arise from this is to try to function as God ourselves. I wrongly believe that life would be better with me in charge. But as Christians, shouldn't our view of God be different? Shouldn't we trust the One who saved us?

Satan works overtime to convince us that God is not as good as He claims to be. This was the lie he used to deceive Adam and Eve. When we question the goodness of God, we take charge. Then, when things don't go so well, our distrust of God is reinforced. We believe He let us down or doesn't care. We become even more convinced that we can't really trust Him.

Maybe our head knows better, but our heart struggles. We may have learned one thing in Sunday school, but we believe life has revealed to us a different lesson. Subtly, we've come to believe things about God that aren't true.

Where does all this confusion start? In many cases, the wrong beliefs we hold about God were introduced to us at home.

Moving Out ... Moving On

But then we leave home and take those beliefs with us. What happens after we leave our family of origin? Let's just say the learning doesn't stop when we leave home. How we view ourselves, and what beliefs we hold about God, impact almost every major decision we make. This in turn often reinforces our misbeliefs.

For example, you leave home feeling devalued or disappointed, as if you never measured up. Your desire to prove something or to be somebody may determine your career path. It may determine the house you buy or the car you drive. Perhaps you're exhausting yourself trying to prove you have value because you didn't feel valued growing up. Maybe you're still trying to win the approval of a parent, even as an adult. Sometimes we're even trying to win the approval of a parent who is no longer living.

What we believe about ourselves impacts who we marry. It's been my experience over the years that wounded people often find wounded people to marry. For some, the decision is simply not to marry. Anger, bitterness, or disappointment carried into adulthood can determine lifestyle choices. As adults, we can find ourselves reacting against or acquiescing to wrong beliefs about ourselves and God—beliefs formulated at home.

How we treat our spouse or parent our children often reflects our experiences in our family of origin. It's very easy to pass along misbeliefs about God to others around us without realizing we are doing so. You can't pass on a right view of God if you don't have a right view of God.

These experiences can reinforce faulty views of God. For example, if we emerge from our family of origin with unresolved wounds or feeling devalued, we may end up with a partner who treats us accordingly. This only serves to further wound and devalue us, which gets projected onto God (and our own children). We unconsciously determine that God must think we're a loser too. Every failure only adds to this conclusion.

These beliefs then impact our parenting. For example, how many parents are using their kids to try to meet unmet needs in their own lives? As parents, our hurts from the past can come out in less-than-productive ways, passing that hurt on to others. This also affects all our other relationships. That impacts how we are treated in return, which again only confirms what we already believe about ourselves. The lies can pile up quickly.

We think God must be disgusted or angry with us. We interpret every bad circumstance as God punishing us or giving us what we deserve. Perhaps we find ourselves desperately trying to appease God to avoid getting clobbered. This may cause us to be angry or afraid of God. He becomes someone to be avoided rather than our place of refuge. This again only serves to reinforce beliefs about God that aren't true.

Our messed-up view of God shows up in many ways as adults. For example, some people exhaust themselves trying to please a God they believe is never satisfied. They believe this because they grew up with a parent who was never satisfied—who probably also grew up with a parent who was never satisfied. They never measured up, no matter how hard they tried.

This is often what drives religion. People are trying and trying to satisfy God, but they never really feel accepted by Him. They are unable to rest in the presence of God because they feel they haven't done enough or haven't done well enough. How can you rest in a God who is never satisfied? How can you trust a God who always seems annoyed at you?

Others fear the wrath of God. God feels unsafe. They fear He may go off on them at any moment. How can you feel safe with a God who feels so unpredictable?

Some have grown up in an environment of ungrace, so they view God accordingly. Ernest Hemingway was a literary genius. He was also a victim of some bad theology at home.

Hemingway knew about the ungrace of families. His devout parents detested Hemingway's libertine life, and after a time his mother refused to allow him in her presence. One year for his birthday, she mailed him a cake along with the gun his father had used to kill himself. Another year she wrote him a letter explaining that a mother's life is like a bank. "Every child that is born to her enters the world with a large and prosperous bank account, seemingly inexhaustible.... The child," she continued, "makes withdrawals but no deposits during the early years. Later, when the child grows up, it is his responsibility to replenish the supply he has drawn down." Hemingway's mother then proceeded to spell out all the specific ways in which Ernest should be making "deposits to keep the account in good standing": flowers, fruit or candy, a surreptitious paying of Mother's bills, and above all a determination to stop "neglecting your duties to God and your Savior, Jesus Christ." Hemingway never got over his hatred for his mother and for her Savior.[1]

I'm sorry to say it, but Hemingway never successfully separated the true Savior from the one depicted by his mother. By this point in the book, you probably know that it's fair to assume his mother struggled with her own faulty view of God too, likely carried over from *her* family growing up. As far as we know, Hemingway went to his grave believing things about Jesus that were not true. God's not like that. What a tragedy. How he would have loved the grace and mercy of the true Savior!

Some people have experienced physical or emotional abuse at home. Some have endured the unwillingness of a parent to prevent or stop such abuse. Perhaps you trusted a parent to protect you but instead ended up exposed and vulnerable. Perhaps you were abused as a child and cried out for help, only to be ignored or shamed into silence.

Is it any surprise, then, that you now feel that God is powerless or unwilling to act in times of crisis? You wonder where God is in times of need. Maybe God feels like that abusive or unresponsive parent, so you protect yourself by not trusting God. You distance yourself from God. Most often, these emotions and beliefs are buried deep in our subconscious. We're not aware of why we feel the way we feel. We just know we struggle to trust God.

People who tend toward control or manipulation are that way for a reason. Somewhere along the way, often at home, they learned that bad things happened when certain situations got out of control. Parents fought or divorced. One parent abused the other. Sexual abuse. Disease ravaged the home. Maybe it was the trauma of moving repeatedly and never having any say in the decision.

Whatever the situation was, it was out of control and, as a result, you got hurt. The solution? Try to control and manipulate the environment to prevent more pain. Remember, if you tend toward control, you are controlling for a reason. Usually, that reason roots back to something hurtful, often at home.

By definition, God is completely uncontrollable. His ways are not our ways, and sometimes it's impossible to make sense out of what He does or allows. Controllers struggle to trust God because God is the ultimate uncontrollable. People feel that if they yield control, if they surrender, bad things will happen. It feels too risky to surrender to God. Simply stated, God can't be trusted.

Words Have a Context

Imagine the courage it would take to believe something as abstract as "God loves you" if you've never really been loved. Sometimes in premarital counseling, I'll ask a couple if they've ever really been deeply loved by someone. It's sobering how often people confess that they feel like they've never really experienced that kind of love. They are hopeful that the person they are marrying will love them that way, but they know they are entering uncharted waters.

When people like that hear that God loves them, what does it mean to them? What do they compare it to? What should they expect? Words that describe God are originally learned and defined, correctly or incorrectly, in a context. Of course, that context is different for each person.

For example, let's say the preacher declares, "God is love." How love was experienced in your home created a filter for your understanding of love. Perhaps for you, love means pleasing someone or keeping secrets or covering things up. Or maybe love was viewed as loyalty over integrity, so love meant you were expected to lie if necessary to protect the family. Maybe love meant keeping your mouth shut or doing what you were told or taking the blame for someone else or enabling destructive behaviors. So, what do you hear when you hear that God is love? Five people may hear five different things.

There are so many words that describe who you are in Christ. Wonderful, truthful, powerful words. But simply repeating a list of words and phrases written on a piece of paper doesn't necessarily clarify or correct misperceptions. The preacher can say, "God loves you," every week but that doesn't mean love is rightly understood. Does God love me like my dad loved me?

Sometimes we underestimate how hard it is for some people to make sense of the words used to describe God. Maybe it's not as clear as we think. Perhaps some of us take a lot for granted and fail to realize the advantages we may have had growing up. Before we cast stones at others who struggle to believe, we need to appreciate how different their story may have been from ours.

Contrast the struggler with someone who has grown up in a secure, loving home. That would certainly be my story. I always knew my parents had an undying love for each other and for me. Even when we went through those awkward stages parents and teenagers go through, I never doubted their love for me.

I never felt I had to perform for my parents or measure up for them. They loved me the same if I was obedient or disobedient. They accepted me just the same whether I had a good game or a bad game. They were proud of me because I was their child, not because of anything I accomplished.

As I grew up, I began to learn about God's love for me. I learned He loves me unconditionally and accepts me as I am in Christ. These concepts made sense to me because I had experienced them with my parents. I'm secure in my relationship with God because I was secure in my relationships at home. I don't distrust God because I didn't have reason to distrust my parents.

They were good teachers. They taught me about God through how they treated me and how they lived.

Think of the home's potential to teach a child—for better or worse—their beliefs related to grace, forgiveness, trust, love, compassion, kindness, reliability, faithfulness, service, submission, leadership, power, justice, fairness, mercy, and so on. Home is the primary teaching environment we experience growing up. It's where our first and foundational beliefs about God come from. It is God's seminary. It is where God is experienced and introduced to the next generation. The question is, what did you learn?

Two Considerations

There are two things to consider here. One is to remember that our family of origin was made up of people with their own stories. They may have been doing the best they could, given the unresolved issues in their own lives. It's not uncommon that these hurts and patterns get passed on from generation to generation. They're not trying to be bad parents—they may simply have had their own pain and struggles that held them in bondage in ways they still don't realize or aren't willing to face. If you want grace and mercy for your story, you must be willing to extend the same to your family of origin.

I realize for some people, this will not come easy. I have shed many tears as I've sat and listened to horror stories of things done to young children. Your story may be so very hard. It may be horrible. No one is suggesting that you shrug off what was done to you as if it were no big deal. But working toward a heart of compassion and forgiveness is the right thing to do. It reflects a right view of God. It is a necessary part of the healing process.

Secondly, we can choose to do better for our generation and the one after that. If you want to do better for your marriage or kids or friends, you have to do the hard work of identifying and correcting beliefs about God that aren't true. It's not enough to simply acknowledge our hurts or point to where someone did us wrong. It's unproductive to cast blame on others, creating further pain. You must resolve to face faulty beliefs about God and get them corrected. This must include examining what you learned about God from your family of origin.

> **Home is where our first and foundational beliefs about God come from. It is God's seminary. The question is, what did you learn?**

Think of it this way: If you experienced hurtful things growing up, then shouldn't you be motivated to do things differently for others? Don't repeat the pattern. Be honest with yourself: Are you repeating the same patterns ... or creating a new legacy? The default mode will be to repeat hurtful patterns, unless you make a determined effort to make changes.

My hope is that as you formulate a more accurate view of God, your heart will more and more resemble the love and compassion of Jesus. I would expect forgiveness from you more than bitterness, mercy more than blame, and a healing of wounds you've already carried too long.

This is your chance to break a cycle and begin a new legacy.

Check It Out!

One question that is sure to arise is how to know if you hold wrong beliefs about God. How do I know if I'm misunderstanding God or defining words incorrectly? That's an important question. Typically, the problem is not that we hold wrong beliefs in our conscious thoughts. We tend to sort those out through reading the Word and biblical instruction. Where we get into trouble is when those beliefs are buried deeply in our subconscious. They tend to show up more in our emotions. Sometimes, we are simply unaware that we hold beliefs about God that aren't true.

We struggle, but we don't know why. You may get all the answers right on a Bible quiz, but that doesn't mean your beliefs about God are accurate. I've known countless people who have a head full of Bible knowledge but have a messed-up view of God.

I believe that once we become aware of wrong beliefs, we can correct them quite quickly. This is not an issue of rebellion, in which we are determined to reject the truth about God. It's an issue of being deceived by lies that need to be corrected. The very essence of being deceived is that you think what you believe is true, but it's not. Therefore, the starting place is to identify what you really believe about God deep in your heart. You need to identify the lies to correct them.

First, there is a need for a standard, a basis for truth. God reveals Himself in the Bible. It is His self-revelation. That must be the starting place. God has given every believer His Spirit to guide us to truth (John 14:16–17) and His Word as a lamp to our feet and a light to our path (Ps. 119:105). But just telling people to read the Bible more doesn't usually clear things up without some help.

God's Not Like That is intended to help you focus on very specific and practical areas related to your family of origin. What did God intend for you to experience at home, and what did you experience in reality? I've hoped to show you the authentic version, and from that you have to identify the counterfeit.

Your emotions often operate like the warning lights on the dashboard of your car. They alert you to beliefs about God that require attention. Ask yourself what aspects of God's character seem to create a negative emotional response in you. Why do you look away when the preacher speaks of God's love? Why do you stop singing when the lyrics of the song keep repeating the message that God is good all the time? Why does it sometimes feel like your brain wants to believe something, but your heart won't go there?

Investigate those emotions. Why do you feel that way? When certain truths about God are revealed or talked about, do you react a certain way? Do you laugh uncomfortably or roll your eyes or find yourself saying something cynical when certain truth claims about God are made? What specific truths about God seem to push your buttons?

Sometimes it's helpful to do this kind of study with a small group of believers who can help you process what you may be missing. Over the years, I've had many conversations with people who have odd reactions to some particular truth about God. I'll stop them and point out what they just said or did and ask why. Often, they are unaware that they reacted as they did. This is where a friend or small group can really help identify reactions or responses you might miss. Of course, many have found help from a Christian therapist or counselor, as well.

> **I believe that once we become aware of wrong beliefs, we can correct them quite quickly.**

Take the time to go back through your written reflections in this book. Ask the Holy Spirit to guide you to truth, and He will faithfully do so. "But when He, the Spirit of truth, comes, He will guide you into all the truth" (John 16:13). God longs for you to know Him as He is. He is delighted to answer that prayer. Identifying wrong beliefs is the critical first step toward a right view of God.

I want to make it clear that I'm not talking about wallowing around in the past, using it as an excuse for poor choices today. I'm talking about a very deliberate attempt to identify wrong beliefs about God and correct them.

I love the story of Jephthah. Listen to the opening lines of his story from Judges 11:

> Now Jephthah the Gileadite was a valiant warrior, but he was the son of a prostitute. And Gilead had fathered Jephthah. Gilead's wife bore him sons; and when his wife's sons grew up, they drove Jephthah out and said to him, "You shall not have an inheritance in our father's house, for you are the son of another woman." So Jephthah fled from his brothers and lived in the land of Tob; and worthless men gathered around Jephthah, and they went wherever he did. (vv. 1–3)

That's a rather abrupt introduction. On the positive side, he was a great warrior. On the negative side, his mom was a prostitute. Even his own half brothers didn't want anything to do with him. Gilead was Jephthah's father. One can only imagine the pain Gilead's wife felt every time she saw Jephthah, the son of a prostitute. Her pain most likely became the force behind Jephthah's rejection.

He was driven out of his own home, and so he chose to befriend "worthless fellows." Jephthah was running with a bad crowd. Sadly, that story sounds all too familiar. Often how we feel about ourselves has a lot to do with who we think will accept us. Those who feel like losers are often drawn to others who feel the same way about themselves. The future for Jephthah looked bleak at best.

Now let's peek at another reference to Jephthah:

> And what more shall I say? For time will fail me if I tell of Gideon, Barak, Samson, Jephthah, of David and Samuel and the prophets, who by faith conquered kingdoms, performed acts of righteousness, obtained promises, shut the mouths of lions, quenched the power of fire, escaped the edge of the sword, from weakness were made strong, became mighty in war, put foreign armies to flight. (Heb. 11:32–34)

Do you know where that lineup of names comes from? It's part of the faith hall of fame in Hebrews 11. That's right. Jephthah, who seemed to be headed for disaster, ended up in the faith hall of fame. Not bad!

You can read the full story of Jephthah for yourself in Judges 11–12. He was a courageous man of faith. Somewhere along the way, he was able to rise above his traumatic childhood and trust God to do great things through him. He went from a social outcast to a hall-of-famer.

The same can happen to anyone who is willing to trust God by faith. Anyone who believes God is who He says He is can experience the life Jesus offers.

Let's put away our excuses and rationalizations and get about the business of knowing and trusting God. Right theology—a right view of God—should equip us well to do what He's called us to do. If even the son of a prostitute can be a faith hall-of-famer, so can you.

You can't change the past, but you can rise above it and be different for the next generation. How will you fulfill the biblical role God intended for you? Will you be part of the generation that breaks the downward cycle and charts a new course?

Reflecting
on
My Family of Origin

There is a big difference between dwelling on the past and learning from the past. The past is past. There's no point wishing things were different. They are what they are. You can wish all day long that your life today was different, but it's not. It is what it is today. So, where do we go from here?

Whatever has been in the past is past. Let's learn what we need to learn from it, then let's begin writing a new story. Are you willing to do what is necessary to make this happen? Let's roll up our sleeves and do the hard work of formulating a right view of God.

For the final "Reflecting on My Family of Origin" page, go back through what you have written on the journal entry pages. Think about your view of God before reading this book, then consider a new, corrected view of God. The path ahead will be largely determined by what you choose to believe is true about God. Your feelings will follow in time, but change starts by an act of your will. You have to choose to believe that God tells the truth.

Journal Entry

Write a paragraph describing your Christian life as it has been over the past year. What feelings or emotions have defined you?

Now write a paragraph describing how your life could look if you had a fully biblical view of God and truly trusted Him.

These changes don't come overnight, but over time. My prayer is that a process has begun that will lead to a more accurate view of God. Let's make your final journal entry a prayer that captures whatever is in your heart as you conclude this book. Is there something you need to confess? Do you want to celebrate and give thanks? Is there something specific you want to share with God or ask of Him?

Conclusion

There are so many things about God that I don't understand. I have a long list of questions that I don't think I'll ever get answered. Some people speculate that one day all our questions will be answered by God. I doubt that's the case. I think it's more likely that someday all our questions will be irrelevant. In that glorious moment, when we stand before Jesus face to face, our questions won't matter anymore.

But I'm not referring only to the hard things in life like pain, suffering, and loss. I also have so many questions about why God would intentionally create me (Ps.139:13–14), love me, and send His Son to rescue me. Like all sinners, I have been the Prodigal Son, and He welcomed me home. To the praise of the glory of His grace, He has saved me (Eph. 1:6). He has made me magnificent (Eph. 2:10).

Even more, He hasn't simply given me a ticket to heaven—He also longs to dwell in relationship with me. He wants to be with me. Just stop and ponder that for a moment. The God who created the universe and reigns supreme over all powers … wants to be with you. That's hard to comprehend. Actually, I can't comprehend it. It's mind-blowing.

I think the evidence that we struggle to believe this is that we spend so little time pursuing God. If we really believed that God is like the father of the Prodigal Son, we'd chase after Him with all our hearts. We know the words and we've heard the claims, but I think we struggle to believe it's really true. I really do believe God longs to be with me more than I long to be with Him.

Wow, it's hard to even write those words. But it is true. God wants to be with me.

How do I know? God said so (John 14:1–6; 17:3, 13, 20–21; Eph. 5; Rev. 19: 7–8). As a matter of fact, He's so committed to this desire that He gave up His Son to make a way back so we could spend forever with Him in paradise. The whole thing just seems so outrageous.

The question is, do you believe it? Do you believe that God wants to be with you? I mean, do you really believe it to such a degree that you experience the freedom that comes only from knowing and believing the truth?

This belief is at the core of our understanding of the purpose of the family. From the very beginning, God created us in His image *so that we can know Him.* He wants to be known, and He wants to know us.

He's so committed to this that He created and designed the family for this purpose. He created the family as the ultimate learning environment to facilitate our ability to know Him. Even before the fall, God put in place a laboratory where people made in His image could begin to understand what it means to experience a soul-satisfying relationship with Him. Family is meant to be the place where we learn to dance with God.

When done correctly, the family is the most powerful environment for learning a right view of God. However, when done poorly, we learn many things about God that aren't true. A messed-up view of God will always be a roadblock to the abundant life Jesus offers.

Let me say it one final time: everyone emerges from their family of origin with a view of God. There are no exceptions. God created the family to work that way. The real question is, "What did you learn?"

Our desire is not to blame our families for our problems today or to disrespect the family we grew up in. That would be displeasing to God. Rather, the intent is to identify and correct things you learned about God that aren't true. The end goal is a right view of God.

This is not an easy assignment. It often takes years to determine what is true and what is messed up about your view of God. So often, these beliefs are buried deep in your subconscious mind. You struggle with God but are unable to figure out why.

Little by little, with the Holy Spirit guiding you through the process, you can identify and correct a faulty view of God. You can sort this out one step at a time. There is every reason for encouragement and hope.

My prayer is that you not only formulate a right view of God but that you pass that view along to the next generation. It's hard to imagine anything more significant to devote your life to than perpetuating the kingdom of God from generation to generation. If you don't think you have the energy to do this hard work for your own benefit, at least be willing to do it for the next generation. You can't pass on a right view of God if you yourself don't have a right view of God. You can do this.

"You will know the truth, and the truth will set you free" (John 8:32).

Notes

Chapter 2: Designed That Way

1. See Victor P. Hamilton, *Book of Genesis: Chapters 1–17* (Grand Rapids, MI: Eerdmans, 1990), 153; and C. F. Keil and F. Delitzsch, *Commentary on the Old Testament*, vol. 1 (Grand Rapids, MI: Eerdmans, 1980), 74–81.

2. Eugene H. Merrill, ed., *The Bible Knowledge Key Word Study: Genesis–Deuteronomy* (Colorado Springs: Victor, 2003), 46.

3. Merrill, *Bible Knowledge Key Word*, 46.

4. C. F. Keil and F. Delitzsch, *Commentary on the Old Testament*, vol. 6 (Grand Rapids, MI: Eerdmans, 1980), 76–81; Frank E. Gaebelein, ed., *The Expositor's Bible Commentary: Volume 2 (Genesis–Numbers)* (Grand Rapids, MI: Zondervan, 1990), 41; and Kenneth A. Mathews, *The New American Commentary: Genesis 1–11:26* (Nashville, TN: Broadman and Holman, 1996), 201.

5. Merrill, *Bible Knowledge Key Word*, 48.

6. Merrill, *Bible Knowledge Key Word*, 48.

7. Timothy Keller, *The Reason for God* (New York: Dutton, 2008), 215.

8. Merrill, *Bible Knowledge Key Word*, 49; and W. E. Vine, Merrill F. Unger, and William White Jr., *Vine's Complete Expository Dictionary of Old and New Testament Words* (Nashville, TN: Thomas Nelson, 1996), 37.

Chapter 4: An Unattractive Jesus

1. Scot McKnight, *The NIV Application Commentary: 1 Peter* (Grand Rapids, MI: Zondervan, 1996), 186.

2. Edmund P. Clowney, *The Message of 1 Peter: The Way of the Cross* (Leicester, UK: Inter-Varsity Press, 1988), 133–34.

3. John R. W. Stott, *The Message of 1 Timothy and Titus* (Leicester, UK: Inter-Varsity Press, 1996), 98.

Chapter 5: Why Do I Struggle with the Church?

1. Archibald Thomas Robertson, *Word Pictures in the New Testament*, vol. 6 (Grand Rapids, MI: Baker, 1931), 544–45.

2. Robertson, *Word Pictures*, 544.

Chapter 6: Where Do I Go in Times of Need?

1. Curt Thompson, MD, psychiatrist, author, and speaker, www.CurtThompsonMD.com. *The Soul of Desire*, *The Soul of Shame*, and *Anatomy of the Soul*.

2. Nancy Pearcy, *Love Thy Body* (Ada, MI: Baker Books, 2018), 127.

3. D. Ross Campbell, *How to Really Love Your Child* (Colorado Springs: David C Cook, 2015), 50–51.

4. For examples and more information, see: "The Importance of Nurture in Child Development" by James M. Slusher; "Nurturing: A Critical Life Skill for Parents and Caregivers" by Gail Innis; "The Dual Role of Parents: Providing Nurture and Structure" by Center for Parenting Education; "Do Parents Matter? Nature vs. Nurture" by Focus on the Family; and "Nature vs. Nurture" by Pennsylvania State University.

5. Campbell, *How to Really Love Your Child*, 55.

Chapter 7: Why Do I Feel So Wounded by God?

1. Paul C. Vitz, *Faith of the Fatherless: The Psychology of Atheism* (Dallas: Spence, 1999), 57.

2. Frank E. Gaebelein, ed., *The Expositor's Bible Commentary: Volume 5 (Psalms–Song of Songs)* (Grand Rapids, MI: Zondervan, 1991), 907; C. F. Keil and F. Delitzsch, *Commentary on the Old Testament*, vol. 6 (Grand Rapids, MI: Eerdmans, 1980), 59–60; Warren Baker and Eugene Carpenter, *The Complete Word Study Dictionary: Old Testament* (Chattanooga, TN: AMG, 2003), 582; and Bruce K. Waltke, *The Book of Proverbs: Chapters 1–15* (Grand Rapids, MI: Eerdmans, 2004), 175–76.

3. Spiros Zodhiates, comp. and ed., *The Complete Word Study Dictionary: New Testament* (Iowa Falls, IA: World Bible, 1992), 1088.

Chapter 8: Wait, God Did What?

1. Philip D. Yancey, *What's So Amazing about Grace?* (Grand Rapids, MI: Zondervan, 1997), 15.

2. W. E. Vine, *A Comprehensive Dictionary of the Original Greek Words with Their Precise Meanings for English Readers* (McLean, VA: MacDonald, 1948), 624–26.

3. John H. Walton, *Old Testament Theology for Christians: From Ancient Context to Enduring Belief* (Downers Grove, IL: IVP Academic, 2017), 68–69.

4. John R. W. Stott, *The Message of Ephesians: God's New Society* (Leicester, UK: Inter-Varsity Press, 1979), 84; James Strong, *The Exhaustive Concordance of the Bible* (McLean, VA: MacDonald, 1981), 27; and R. Kent Hughes, *Ephesians: The Mystery of the Body of Christ* (Wheaton, IL: Crossway Books, 1990), 81–82.

5. F. F. Bruce, *The Epistle to the Ephesians: A Verse-by-Verse Exposition* (London: Pickering and Inglis, 1973), 52.

6. Bruce, *Epistle to the Ephesians*, 40.

7. See Isaiah 49:14–16; 62:3; Zephaniah 3:17; 1 Peter 2:9; 1 John 3:1.

Chapter 9: Afterwards

1. Philip D. Yancey, *What's So Amazing about Grace?* (Grand Rapids, MI: Zondervan, 1997), 38.